The Ultimate Deployment Guidebook

Insight into the Deployed Soldier and a Guide for the First-Time Deployed

Paul N. Smith
SFC Kristina A. Smith

Savas Beatie
California

Library of Congress Cataloging-in-Publication Data

Smith, Paul N.
The ultimate deployment guidebook : insight into the deployed soldier and a guide for the first-time deployed / Paul N. Smith, SFC Kristina A. Smith. -- First edition.
    pages cm
Includes bibliographical references and index.
ISBN 978-1-61121-142-9 (pbk.)
    1. United States--Armed Forces--Military life--Handbooks, manuals, etc. 2. United States--Armed Forces--Military life--Humor 3. Deployment (Strategy)--Handbooks, manuals, etc. 4. Deployment (Strategy)--Humor I. Smith, Kristina A. II. Title.
    U766.S65 2013
    355.1'294--dc23
    2013031056

First edition, first printing, 2013

Published by
Savas Beatie LLC
989 Governor Drive, Suite 102
El Dorado Hills, California 95762

Phone: 916-941-6896
Email: sales@savasbeatie.com
Website: www.savasbeatie.com

Savas Beatie titles are available at special discounts for bulk purchases in the United States by corporations, institutions, and other organizations. For more details, please contact Special Sales, P.O. Box 4527, El Dorado Hills, CA 95762, e-mail us at sales@savasbeatie.com, or visit our website at www.savasbeatie.com for additional information.

Printed in the United States of America.
Cover photo courtesy of iStockphoto.
All photos courtesy of authors unless otherwise noted.

Paul N. Smith

I would like to dedicate this book to all of our military personnel who make the day in and day out sacrifices to our Country.

SFC Kristina A. Smith

I would like to dedicate this book to my grandma "GG" who continues to ensure I am blessed from above.

Disclaimer

Although this book may be the best piece of literary art you will ever lay your wandering eyes upon, the two individuals responsible for it are just that: individuals. The contents of this book are merely the opinions and random musings of the authors, and should in no way be considered to reflect official Army doctrine or rules.

Contents

Contents (continued)

**Part 3
What We Live For**

Preface

How All of this Came to Be

So, I was in my first year overseas as a contractor. I was sitting in the wonderful Base Defense Operations Center (BDOC), assuming my eight-hour-a-day duties as the BDOC battle captain for the day shift, helping out the awesome American soldier. At that moment I realized, wow: between my previous deployment here as a soldier and this deployment as a civilian, I've seen and done a ton of things that I wouldn't have otherwise. Some of those things are obvious, others less so—as you'll realize if you keep reading.

Then, that same day I was meeting some of the BDOC crew for the first time—and Sergeant First Class (SFC) Smith brought up the same subject! She was talking about all of the weird things she had seen on the cameras. For instance, she said she saw a guy bathing in a ditch by the side of the highway. She asked, who does that—it only happens downrange, right?

So the two of us started talking about all the different things we do and see only during deployment. Then we decided to make a list. At first it was just fun to see how many points we could come up with. But the list kept growing and growing. We came up with the main points over a three-day period, and added the rest over the following weeks.

I started thinking to myself, hey, we could make a story out of all these points, or even a book, and SFC Smith agreed. We started typing away, covering the points we'd listed ourselves, plus stuff we'd heard from other people, and personnel stories in general.

After a while, I really started to talk to SFC Smith. I said, hey, this has real potential—let's actually write a book! I said, I'm no talented writer or anything, but some of this stuff is both hilarious and insightful into the life of a soldier or civilian contractor overseas. We thought people would get a kick out of reading what we were putting together. And we had something that most similar efforts don't: two points of view on the same story—especially because one is the female and the other the male. (I knew I could not, on any level, talk about the female aspect; I'm not going to say she couldn't talk about the male aspect, but I felt I had a little more insight into the mind of the male soldier—for obvious reasons.)

What started with making a list became, over time, a real journey of discovery. We hope this book is informative for you—and as fun to read as it was to write.

Paul and Kristina on an overseas deployment.

Introduction

This book has three parts, broadly covering:

1. Why We're Here

2. How We Live

3. What We Live For

Within those three parts are nine chapters, covering everything from food to free time to firepower. Built into the chapters are a lot of breakout boxes covering specific topics. In addition to the chapters of the main text, you'll find a lot of the book's content in the appendices. (Remember, this book started off as a bunch of lists.) In general, the chapters contain a lot of Paul's and Kristina's thoughts and experiences, while the appendices contain a lot of information both from them and other sources. Again, in a general way, the appendices have more to do with *The Ultimate Deployment Guidebook* aspect of the book, whereas the main text covers more of the *Insight into the Deployed Soldier* aspect. We think both the main text and the appendices are well worth reading—don't skip either one! However, if you're looking for information on a particular subject, consult the table of contents and/or the index. Also, while we explain some acronyms and other military jargon along the way, there's a glossary/acronym list at the back of the book so you can look up any terms you might need explained.

We've made it simple for anyone reading this book to understand who wrote which parts, but it wasn't a matter of giving credit. We did it to make sure that, when a story is being told from a female point of view, you don't think Paul hid spy cameras in the female tents and shower facilities! So when you see this symbol (♂), that section comes from Paul Smith, and when you see this one (♀), that section comes from SFC Kristina Smith.

Over the course of the book we refer to General Order #1 several times. The armed services issue directives regarding expected standards of conduct for personnel deployed to forward areas. General Order #1 applies to all U.S. military personnel while present in the theater of operation.

Acknowledgments

From Kristina

I would like to thank my publisher, all of my family, and friends for their continued support. A special thanks to all of the men and women who have ever served in the U.S. Armed Forces.

From Paul

I would like to thank everyone from my previous unit A 1/10 CAV and a special dedication to my support line Kristi Smith.

Part 1

Why We're Here

Chapter 1

War: Keeping Ourselves Alive

Why you may be surrounded by sand and water, yet you're not at the beach . . .

♀

Ah, the smell of the ocean, the sound of waves crashing, and the feeling of sand between your toes. In every direction you look, young, hard bodies in bikinis and shorts are splashing around in the ocean. You watch the water drip down a chiseled body, from the chest all the way down the legs. You're on the world's greatest beach.

Wake up, soldier! When they said you were going to "the sandbox," that's not what they meant. What did you think you were going to do, spend a day in the life of David Hasselhoff? This isn't *Baywatch*, soldier, it's the U.S. Army. We don't play in the sand, we live in the sand, we work in the sand, and we destroy things that walk on the sand!

The closest you'll get to the beach vision described above is being next to a rain puddle with your battle buddy in his or her physical fitness uniform. However, you can have all the water you want—to drink, that is: there are bottles of water on large pallets in every living area and strategically placed throughout the forward operating base (FOB). And you might even see a palm tree! So, drink up, soldier, and welcome to paradise!

Why you'll contemplate which is hotter: the temperature outside or the gates of hell . . .

♀

I have to be honest and admit I've never read Dante's *Inferno*. So, I'm not sure whether he made a reference to the temperature in each of the different levels of hell. I'm pretty sure if he did, he didn't express it in degrees Fahrenheit or Celsius.

Let's calibrate by saying that on a mild summer day downrange, the sun blazes down and begins to fry you like an egg cracked over a Texas sidewalk in August. In the shade, it's "only" 110 degrees.

The typical soldier's load includes a weapon, ammunition, helmet, body armor, and sometimes a rucksack. The total combat load for a soldier can weigh 40 pounds to more than 130 pounds, depending on the mission and the soldier's duty position.

Carrying the combat load adds 10 degrees to a soldier's body temperature. Boots start sticking to the roadways, and that bottle of water you had in your cargo pocket is hot in less than 30 minutes. Now that's hot!

Why you'll be excited for the cold season (because that's when the fighting season ends) . . .

♂

As far as "the fighting season" is concerned, don't misunderstand. It's not that fighting only occurs during a certain time of year. But the level does drop significantly when the temperature does. In some places, especially in Afghanistan, you can even get snow in the desert.

One of my favorite sayings is, "Terrorists have schedules." For the most part, they work between the hours of 8:00 a.m. and 4:00 p.m., and they usually take the winter off. Maybe the reasons are weather-related, or maybe it's just the best time to rest.

The worst part about this is that right before the rainy/snowy/cold season starts, the terrorists seem to feel they have to jam their last few good attacks into the remaining week or two. The running joke here is that they have to fire off all their munitions before the next fiscal year or else they won't get as much money next year. We all know how horrible that would be!

Why even a claustrophobic person might run into an enclosed cement structure packed full of people elbow to elbow . . .

♂

Imagine you're overseas on a U.S. base. Out of nowhere, mortars and rockets start hitting the base. You'll do one of two things:

1. Run to the nearest bunker. There you will find a LOT of other people, and you will end up sitting or standing next to some of the smelliest people anywhere on earth. You will remain there for 20 minutes or longer until the all-clear is given.

2. Fall to the floor, cover your head, and pray that NOT joining the mad, frenzied run to the bunkers is a better decision.

Why every day will be like the 4th of July, except without the picnic blankets and fried chicken . . .

♀

What's really fun and awesome is to watch the rocket launch over your head, while hearing all the oohs and aahs! That is, until you see that it's about to land right behind you. Then "That's awesome!" changes to "Oh, crap—incoming!"

Most of the time—and I do say most of the time, because nothing is 100 percent effective against anything—the loudspeaker will alert the FOB to its impending doom by announcing the incoming attack. What's crazy is that most FOB veterans don't go running to the bunkers; they're so conditioned to the announcement that they don't even bother to roll out of bed when the alarm sounds. Some have the attitude, "If it's going to hit, it's going to hit, and there's nothing I can do about it." To quote my favorite saying, "It is what it is!" That's until you actually see the rocket fly over your head, or the impact site just happens to be within 100 meters of your tent. That's when the word "Incoming!"—there's a rocket headed in your direction, dummy!—actually sinks in.

For me, the most memorable attack occurred one morning when the insurgents attacked the FOB where I was stationed in Iraq. I was sitting on the toilet in our military working dog (MWD) kennels reading a *Stars and Stripes*, which gives you an indication of what I was doing. The next thing I knew, BOOM! The explosion was so massive it blew the windows open with such force I thought they were going to break on impact. It rattled the whole building.

What I did immediately after the explosion still doesn't make sense to me to this day: I looked down. It was as if I thought what caused the explosion had somehow come out of my behind. As soon as I realized it hadn't, I cleaned myself up and went outside.

To my surprise, I saw a massive smoke cloud in the direction of one of our Iraqi brethren bases, and helicopters taking flight in that direction. Not too long after that, another vehicle-borne improvised explosive device (VBIED) went off at another Iraqi base adjacent to us. But it wasn't until I heard the tower guards firing that it dawned on me: huh, they never do that—we must be under attack!

I used to sit outside during the day reading a book while hearing hundreds, if not thousands, of rounds fired, as well as various explosions going off. All I can say is, it's like reading a book while the television is on: somehow you manage to concentrate even though there's that annoying background noise. Most soldiers downrange become so conditioned to the sound of gunfire and explosions that they're immune to it. It becomes like trying to read with the TV on: it's not until your spouse comes in and tells you it's time for dinner— or you hear the announcement "Rocket attack!"—that you lift your head up. I know it's almost unbelievable, but it's true.

Why you'll find yourself making bets about what time the rockets will hit each day . . .

♂

Most of you readers won't be able to personally identify with this— at least yet—but for those of you who've been on one of "those" FOBs/combat outposts (COPs)/patrol bases: you just knew what day or time of day the rockets or mortars were coming in.

Those who are too sick to realize that placing bets—whether monetary or not—on how many rockets were coming in are just screwed-up individuals. It gets really bad when the betting starts to concentrate on where the mortar or rocket is actually going to hit each day.

♀

Not only do soldiers make bets as to what time the rockets will hit, but they also plan their day around it. For instance, I was temporarily located in a place that received indirect fire (IDF) between 1830 and 1930 every day. I was in charge of the group I was traveling with, so I was responsible for reporting the accountability of all the soldiers after we received IDF. To complete this task, I would ensure I ate dinner and was back in my tent by 1820. I could not deliver my report in my physical fitness uniform, so I had to stay in my duty uniform until after I reported our accountability, which ended up being sometime later in the evening. So every evening between 1830 and 1930 I would just lie in my bunk waiting for the attack.

One morning, one of my fellow noncommissioned officers (NCOs) asked me whether I was going to the United Services Organization (USO) center that evening because they were having a Texas Hold'em Tournament. I happen to be a Texas Hold'em fan, and on my first tour I won a t-shirt for being the first female to make it to the head table. After he asked me that, I gave him a look and we both laughed. I told him, "It's one thing for them to fire rockets at us, but it's quite another when they start messing with my Hold'em. Now it's serious!"

Why the saying "What doesn't kill you makes you stronger" will come to make sense in so many ways . . .

♂

By this point, if you've been paying attention, I don't think I need to explain why this statement is true. But we do have a couple of cool stories for you.

My first experience with a mortar attack came when I was on a little patrol base called Al Hilla. My buddy Willy B. and I were watching a bootleg copy of some random movie. At about 2230 (10:30 p.m.), the first round suddenly came in. It sounded like a combination of thunder and an earthquake. Almost all of us were new privates, and this was our first experience with a mortar attach. I've never seen a group of people move so quickly: I believe we all had our gear on and were in the bunker right outside our tent in a matter of seconds.

It felt as if we waited inside that bunker forever. Staring into the eyes of my companions, I could see both anxiety and heightened determination. Even though our only experience with these types of scenarios had been in a training setting, it seemed everyone knew what to do. As soon as the all-clear was given, our training took over and people grabbed their gear and headed out to their assigned sections. The NCOs had to give very few orders.

Then an NCO told us we had to man the south tower. Normally this tower was never manned because we trusted our Iraqi Army counterparts to do their jobs, and that tower was right next to their gate.

During our rush to the tower, all that ran through my head was, "This is for real!" Up until that moment, it had just seemed like another training exercise. But I was at ease knowing my good friend Willy would back me up no matter what happened.

We stood up in that tower for what seemed like two hours. The Quick Reaction Force (QRF) went around trying to find the enemy mortar team. We scanned our sectors, watching for anything suspicious or out of place. Finally, after what seemed like an eternity, we were ordered to stand down. The QRF had done its job and the threat had passed. We were able to go back to sleep.

Now, for some of you vets out there, this may not have been the coolest story ever. But for me and the rest of my tent full of brand-new privates, it was probably our biggest adrenaline rush ever.

This experience also made me realize that physical fitness wasn't just about looking good and passing my physical fitness test. Even though we didn't have to run much that night, in order to do well in a combat scenario you need to be at your physical peak. That night, Willy and I made it to the tower in record time and were the first to start scanning for threats. Even so, after that day I put in a lot more time at the gym to make sure I would be ready to meet my next physical demand. Often "What doesn't kill you makes you stronger" should be translated as, "What you're lucky enough to escape only makes you realize you could have been better."

♀

Every soldier who has served downrange has a war story or two. There were the times we received drive-bys, complete with AK-47s and grenades; sometimes an improvised explosive device (IED) would strike a vehicle; and there were the seemingly endless rounds of IDF.

No worries, though: much like the "gangstas" in the states who hold their "gats" (slang for guns) sideways, the insurgents can't shoot either!

It was the experiences I went through during my first deployment that taught me the grace with which I went through the second. Now it's time to get serious! It is imperative that prior to deploying to your theater of operation you become well versed on the enemy's techniques, tactics, and procedures (TTPs). We also recommend that you request a copy of your unit's tactical standard operating procedure (SOP). An outstanding resource to review before you deploy is the Center for Army Lessons Learned (CALL) at http://usacac.army.mil/CA2/call/.

Why you'll get to see a free air show every day . . .

♀

You'll be able to see fighter jets, helicopters, and military transport aircraft from the comfort of your base every day. Why, back in the states, some folks pay $5.00–$15.00 and travel for miles to attend air shows. And downrange, the experience you get is especially intense. Every one of your senses gets taken on a joy ride, every day, for free! The aircrafts are so loud they can wake you out of a dead sleep. The vibrations you feel, even within your tent, are so strong you'll run and stand in the doorway because you'll think you're experiencing a Texas-size quake. At night the aircraft will put on a laser light show, complete with different colored illumination and tracer rounds. Finally, they sometimes drop things from the sky that explode upon impact. Now that's entertainment!

U.S. Helicopter. One of the many birds that we had
coming in and out to help transport troops.

Why the term "pimping out your ride" won't mean what you think . . .

♀

What's up, Xzibit? Sure, MTV broadcasts your successful show around the world, showcasing you customizing cars. But you don't have anything on Uncle Sam!

On the hit show *Pimp my Ride*, they spend some change pimping out hoopties into fly low riders with bling. OK, to translate for the rest of us: they take vehicles that barely run, even vehicles rescued from a junkyard that may have mice living in them, and fix them up. They spend thousands of dollars to replace the upholstery, throw a TV and sound system in there, and slap on a new coat of paint.

Well, Uncle Sam spends tens of thousands of dollars to "pimp out" our vehicles too. Unlike the lucky owners on the TV show however, we don't get a new paint job or upholstery. We do, however, get computers; satellite navigation systems; a weapon system whose controls allow the gunner to engage the enemy while sitting in the back seat of the vehicle; an armor survivability kit; and 18-22-inch rims with run-flat tires. Now what!

Note: The High Mobility Multipurpose Wheeled Vehicle (HMMWV), pronounced "Humvee," has been replaced by the mine-resistant, ambush-protected (MRAP) vehicle in most theaters of operation.

Why your love of traveling may diminish . . .

♀

On my first deployment, I thought I had it all figured out. I found out from other soldiers who had previously deployed that I would have to make several helicopter trips to reach my final destination. These helpful soldiers also attempted to scare me with tales of vomiting and "combat landings." But I'd been fooled by these guys before, and I wasn't buying it, not this time.

On the other hand, I do get seasick on waterbeds and dizzy on merry-go-rounds, and once threw up on a puddle jumper. So, just to be safe, I decided to carry a plastic bag with me. I had an extra grocery sack in my bag because I was traveling with my MWD, and her bowel movements weren't always the most predictable.

I decided I would put the bag in an outside pocket of my assault pack (a fancy name for an Army backpack). The crewmen of the Chinook helicopter gave us a preflight briefing. This was not about where our flotation devices were, or that we should put our tray tables in an upright and locked position. Instead he issued orders as follows: "You will not, and I repeat, you will not throw up on this aircraft. That includes the belly of my chopper. If you find that you have to throw up, you have two choices. Number 1, you can take your helmet off and throw up inside it. Or number 2, you can pull your army combat uniform (ACU) top away from you and throw up inside it."

"Hold up," I thought, "is this guy really telling us that if we have to throw up, we have to throw up on ourselves? Man, that sucks for the rest of these guys if they have to puke! I'm sure glad I was smart enough to come prepared!" The dictionary defines "arrogance" as "showing an offensive attitude of superiority."

I was seated along the wall on the co-pilot's side of the chopper, looking directly across to my MWD, Anna. I was reassuring her that everything was going to be all right and trying to get her to lie down. The helicopter took off, and to my surprise the ride was rather smooth.

The drop ramp was down, and where the tail gunner was sitting behind his weapon, was the world's greatest view. It was the middle of the night, the stars were out, and there was a gentle breeze kissing me in the face. We were flying over the oilfields of Kirkuk, Iraq, and we could see the gas flares at the top of the oil wells. It was completely silent. Right then—that moment, flying in a helicopter in Iraq—was one of the most peaceful moments of my life.

It was soon interrupted by the pilot making an announcement that they were going to turn the computer off and conduct some maneuvers. The following will give you the best idea of the hell I was about to endure: Imagine you're riding in the back seat of a car with a student driver who has failed his driver's exam three times and is now lost. We went up, down, right, and left. Not only was my MWD upchucking, but she also lost all control of her bowels. I closed my eyes and kept telling myself, "Don't puke, don't puke!" Uh oh,

I'm going to puke. I reached for my assault pack—again and again I reached, but my arms were too short, and the seatbelt that was saving my life was also preventing me from reaching the bag. I started to panic a little.

I purposely hadn't eaten dinner and had only drank two bottles of water prior to the flight. I thought, OK, if I throw up right now, it will only be water, and they won't notice water, will they? What a genius! So I threw up on the floor. See, that wasn't too bad. I'm going to be all right! The dictionary defines "karma" as "one's acts, considered as fixing one's lot in future existence. . . ."

Oh no, I'm going to puke again! Why won't they land this dang thing?! There was no way I could throw up on the floor again. I looked around for something, anything—other than my helmet or my shirt—to throw up in. Then I remembered I had my patrol cap (an Army baseball-type hat) in my cargo pocket. I had no other choice. I pulled my patrol cap out and threw up in it—four more times before the bird landed.

They wouldn't let me throw my patrol cap away in the aircraft, but who could blame them? So I had to carry my hat—full of vomit— off the bird. All I could think was, Lord, I hope I never have to fly again. Then the soldier next to me yelled, "Hurry up, we only have an hour 'til our next flight!"

Why it's acceptable to have cool call signs . . .

♀

Somebody has to say it, so I will: in our pursuit of a kinder, gentler society, we've gone too far. As a female soldier, I'm a huge advocate of hostility-free workplaces. However, I also have a pretty good sense of humor. So, even though I'm capable of functioning in environments that are sometimes overly sensitive and overly politically correct, it's nice to have a bit of a break downrange.

In the military we use call signs, handles, and code words for various things. Many Hollywood movies have made this aspect of military procedure famous. (If you don't know about Iceman, Viper, or Maverick, you'd better ask somebody!)

Conducting military operations in a theater of operation can be a very intense and stressful experience for service members. So we all pull together and do our best to keep each other's spirits up. This is important during both long periods of down time and highly stressful moments.

I was having one of those stressed-out moments when I saw the following message: "Be advised, Big Sexy en route to Highway Stripper, time now!" I can't share with you what that actually meant— but does it really matter? The message was priceless on its own!

Why the Army spends so much on fuel . . .

This will tell you something about how the military spends money. The following information is taken directly from an article in *National Defense Magazine* titled "How Much Does the Pentagon Pay for a Gallon of Gas?"

If troops are in hostile areas, prices can range from $100 to $600 for "in-theater" delivery. If the only way to ship fuel is via helicopters, the Army estimates it can cost up to $400 a gallon.

Can you tell me how that makes sense? For what we do, we need more gas than anything else. No wonder it costs so much to go to war—the damn gas is killing our expense budget.

Why a female might attempt to urinate into a bottle while riding in a moving vehicle . . .

The female urination device (FUD) is a funnel-like object that allows female soldiers to urinate while standing up. It's standard issue for some female soldiers deploying to a theater of operation. (You can buy a civilian version in some sporting/outdoor stores or over the internet for between $4.00 – $15.00).

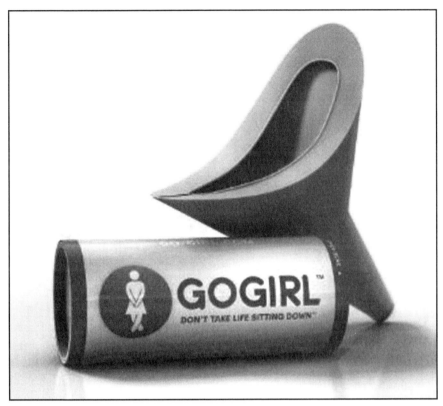

Female Urinary Device. On the road? Are you a female? Look forward
to using your FUD in case you need to go. *http://www.go-girl.com/*

A FUD is most useful while riding in military convoys. Within a
team, there is no gender differentiation as to which soldier is placed
in what position. I've heard tales of a female soldier standing in the
center of a vehicle, simultaneously manning her weapon and urinating
into a FUD, while her male supervisor held an empty water bottle
below it. Wow, talk about "one team, one fight." Hooah!

I could have used a FUD when I was deployed to Iraq. Because I
deployed as an individual augmentee—it was just me and my MWD,
Anna—I didn't get all the perks that females in some other units did.
I'll never forget being out on a mission one day, and having to search
a factory for explosives.

To begin with, let me note that when I first got to Iraq, I tried not
to drink a lot of water while out on mission because I didn't want

to have to use the bathroom. But that theory didn't hold up when temperatures began to exceed 100 degrees.

So, on this mission, there I was in a field, surrounded by combat-arms guys, and I had to pee. I tried to hold it for as long as I possibly could while scouting out some adequate area for me to go. But, unfortunately, it got to a point when I couldn't hold it anymore—I was officially in emergency mode.

The only thing around was part of a wall, about seven feet high. I asked my security team to turn away. I put my back to the wall. I moved Anna in front of me. Then I dropped my drawers.

That moment confirmed for me that Anna and I were really a team, because she stood still in one place the whole time I peed. The guys were laughing, and one of them commented, "Man's best friend, indeed."

Why you may have to depend on cell phone service provided by the other side . . .

♂

Everyone needs a cell phone, right? The war is reaching its latter stages and we have come to trust some of the locals to provide service for us; so it's not uncommon to actually see and use this luxury now, right?

Sure, as long as you don't mind paying about two dollars a minute, you're golden—all the modern conveniences, right at your doorstep.

The additional downside is that you can be pretty sure that whoever is providing your service is also listening in, so you might want to be careful what you say. Even the smallest things can help the enemy out.

Why the Russians get to monitor our internet . . .

♀

In case you didn't know: the Russians have the internet contract with the Afghanis.

Look out, Homeland Security—someone has beaten you to your job! PATRIOT Act, heck—we have trained spies monitoring our internet! Where are all those Cold War vets—we've got Reds in the wire! Right now, on the ocean floor, Boris and Natasha are in a sealed room, sipping vodka while they monitor our Facebook pages for intel on the Russian submarine K-19. They're being aided by that guy from the movie *Taken* and *Indiana Jones*—how could you! Quick, somebody go get former President Bush—we need someone who'll invade Europe!

OK, maybe that's a little on the dramatic side . . . but it's also somewhat true. Keep in mind, the same rules apply that apply to network security back home apply downrange. Make sure you do your part to prevent leaking sensitive information, including your own. If you have any questions, seek out your unit information systems security officer (ISSO) or refer to Department of Defense (DoD) Directives 5200.28, 5200.5, or 5200.19, to name just a few.

Why the phrase "Thank Goodness it's Friday" has no meaning . . .

♀

Like most of my brothers- and sisters-in-arms, I've experienced the daily grind of downrange existence. During my second deployment, I worked 12 hours a day every day. This is not uncommon, and if you add in time for physical fitness for those of us who try to stay in shape, it's more like 14-hour days.

I used to keep track of the days of the week by which tasks I had to do or by what the dining facility (DFAC) was serving that night. Soldiers joke about going to Combat Stress not because they can't handle the war but because they want four days off!

Chapter 2

Battle Buddies, Fobbits, and Allies: Keeping Ourselves Together

Why you'll realize how truly annoying your battle buddies are . . .

♀

Wikipedia defines a battle buddy as a partner assigned to a fellow soldier in the United States armed forces. Matched in pairs, each battle buddy is expected to assist his or her partner, both in and out of combat.

Soldiers have employed the battle buddy concept since the American Revolution. General Nathanael Greene was often considered to be General Washington's right-hand man. A more recent example would be Bubba and Forrest Gump, from basic training until Bubba's tragic death in Vietnam. Your battle buddy is the only one who understands what you're going through, because he or she is right there in the middle of it with you.

The battle buddy concept is one example how we, the service members in the armed forces, have progressed ahead of our civilian counterparts. Remember in the movie *We Were Soldiers Once . . . and Young*, when Lt. Col. Hal Moore addressed the group of soldiers and family members prior to the unit's departure for Vietnam. He said, "Look around you. In the Seventh Cavalry, we've got a captain from the Ukraine. Another from Puerto Rico. We've got Japanese, Chinese, Blacks, Hispanics, Cherokee Indians, Jews and Gentiles— all Americans." If only the rest of the world could have the same tolerance and acceptance we in the armed forces have for one another.

But have you ever been sitting across from someone while he or she was eating chow and realized that everything—from the way he holds his fork to how she chews her food—gets on your last damn nerve? Who taught this guy how to eat? Who slurps their soup like that? You know, you don't have to use your sleeve—there are napkins on the table. Maybe if I push the pile toward her, she'll get the hint. This guy is disgusting; how do I eat with this guy three times a day, every day, without gagging?!

Of course, we females have an innate, natural desire to nurture others. We are more sensitive, thoughtful, and accepting of others. So, when other females come to us with their problems, we are there for them and truly concerned:

- Oh boy, Buck-Tooth Betty's having man troubles again! What, he doesn't appreciate you? Well, maybe he doesn't know you're a Triple Crown winner, Seabiscuit! Every day I have to listen to this heifer go on and on about this loser. Here we go again, she's going to complain about him for hours, then ask me for advice. So I can once again tell her to stop wasting her time with this guy. Oh, she's crying, damn it, and I was going to watch *Bridget Jones' Diary* tonight!

- And here comes Subject Matter Expert (SME) Stephens. Shh, stop talking before he gets over here. I really don't feel like listening to him go on for hours about how he would've done whatever or how he's done it before. What's his Military Occupational Specialty (MOS)? That doesn't matter, he could be a damn plumber, but somehow, some way, he still knows how to build a rocket in his garage! I'm so sick of this guy. Great, he asked Too-Nice Nichols what we were talking about, and of course she's going to tell him. Oh, well, maybe if we just smile every now and again, then break eye contact, he'll shut up. What the h*** (WTH)?! Doesn't this guy know anything about active listening? Nobody's looking at you, guy, and we keep interrupting you to try to change the subject—hint, hint! Boy, I can't wait for this deployment to be over.

• Then there's War-Story Johnson. Man, how does this guy manage to be only 25 years old and in the army for all of six years, but he's the best soldier to have ever served. I've heard all of his "war stories" at least six times. How does he manage to seem to downplay himself even while he's bragging about himself? "Well, I just thought that was something every soldier knew how to do, but it wasn't until the commander 'coined' me that I realized it's not. We were on a hill taking fire when everybody else (a whole platoon of soldiers) just froze, and I had to lead them through the fight. I was like, come on, guys, I'm just a Specialist, you should know what to do!" Well, I guess it's because every male in your family from the dawn of time has served in the armed forces, right? Your father's a command sergeant major, your uncle's a major, and your grandfather stormed the beaches of Normandy. Why, you can trace your family roots back to the *Mayflower*, and they built this country from the ground up. Wow, well, thank goodness for the sacrifices of your family. I don't know how we ever could have made it without them—or you!

• Downer Daniels is in the corner crying again. You would think she was that girl from *The Secret Life of Bees* with a wailing wall, for gosh sakes! How can someone be that damn sad all day, every day, about absolutely nothing? She's been to Combat Stress and the chaplain, and she even receives daily feedback on her blog, "Why Does My Life Suck?" I wonder what she's upset about now? Maybe Sergeant Jones asked her to sweep the floor again, and the stress of it was just too much. Boy, the people they let in the army to serve as "Disciplined Warriors."

I'm sorry I got off topic. As I was saying, if everybody else would just learn from our example of tolerance for others, the world would be a much better place.

Why you'll probably learn way too much about your battle buddy . . .

♀

You probably could have gone the rest of your life without finding out some of the things you learned about your battle buddies and supervisors downrange.

In the rear (back home), at the end of the day, everybody goes their own separate ways. If you're single, maybe you and a couple of buddies go to a club or to the mall (Walmart), and later maybe chill in somebody's room. However, you do eventually part ways. And what the others do at home is their business, and what you do in your room is yours.

Well, not downrange, sister! Downrange, nothing you do is private, and everybody on the FOB knows your business. Here are some things you could have gone the rest of your life without knowing:

- Have you ever been listening to someone tell a story that made you uneasy? You're trying not to look nervous or freaked out as you sit there, but you're wondering, should I tell someone about this? Does an image come to you of the FBI knocking on your door three years from now, asking whether you ever knew this guy?

- There's "Wacko" Williams, who tells tales about aliens taking over the planet, and you're scared because you know he's serious. He keeps making references to *The War of the Worlds*, and how he belongs to an underground group called Project Terminator. He goes on in detail about the many acres of land he owns back in Montana that are a maze of landmines and underground bunkers. The worst part is, he looks truly offended that you don't want to join the resistance.

- Then there's the night you go to borrow one of your battle buddy's movies. You pull back his sheet wall—and realize you'll never be the same again. You see your buddy on his knees, worshiping a naked Malibu Barbie and chanting the Spice Girls hit "Tell Me What You Want, What You Really,

Really Want." Then, the next day he approaches you and tells you he really didn't appreciate you interrupting his religious rituals.

- How about "Pantless" Patterson who comes from a family of nudists. He hates the feeling of clothes on him, and spends as much time naked as possible. The entire tent agrees to never turn the lights on, and live in total darkness for fear of rounding a corner and seeing One-Eyed Willie!

Have you ever wondered whether you're the last sane person on the planet? What if you *are* the last sane person on the planet, and the rest of the world consists of alien pods? Like that stray dog you see on the way to the dining facility every morning: he stops and stares at you, and you feel as if he can see into your soul. Man, I can't wait to re-deploy and get away from all these crazy people!

Have you met the guy yet who incessantly talks about the 2012 end-of-the-world conspiracy theory? DON'T! It doesn't matter what you say: you're wrong, he's right. Even though he wasn't. The end of the world is coming; Armageddon is near. For the low, low cost of half your paycheck for a year, he'll even make room in his bunker out in the middle of Kansas for you and your immediate family. He'll request that you be a part of the monthly teleconference to discuss repairs to the old missile silo where you'll all be living and continue the discussion about how much more canned food you can fit down in the storage facility.

♂

There are some conversational subjects and activities you just shouldn't want to get into with others, even your battle buddies—especially in the shower. This list of reminders is not all-inclusive but following it will definitely keep you from getting your simple-minded self kicked.

Male Shower Etiquette 101

* Do not make eye contact with other males—not even the slightest glance.

* Do not compliment other males while you or they are naked. For example, "Hey, dude, looks like the gym has really been helping you out."

* This should be obvious, but: don't drop the soap. Don't even make jokes about dropping the soap, because no one will think it's as funny as you do.

* Never ask to borrow a washcloth or towel before, during, or after your shower. For whatever reason you think you might need my extra towel, remember it's been all over my butt at some point.

* If you suspect something could be wrong with your "package" (e.g., bumps, drips, rashes), don't ask the other guys to check it out for you. Go to the doctor, man!

* Don't ask for other guys' opinions about the size of your package. We all know our country's average is around six. Just think about your package in those terms, and don't ask me about it.

* If your FOB allows the local national translators to use the same shower facilities as you, immediately leave. Don't even try to figure out what they are saying.

Why someone can make 10 times as much as you for doing the exact same thing . . .

♂

This topic is probably going to be interesting. You see, I myself am one of those horrible contracting civilian types.

What's funny is, the whole time I was in the Army I was always thinking to myself, "Man, I could do that job. Hell, I'm doing most of it right now!"

I can't really give specifics on what contracting civilians do, because I don't want to jeopardize national security. But one that stands out in my mind is the guy—making who knows how much money—who serves me my food at the DFAC.

♀

On my first deployment I was doubling down as both a patrol explosive detection dog (PEDD) handler and a kennel master. Then a civilian kennel master in an undisclosed location made it known to me that he was making a six-figure salary—in a place where no one should be collecting hazardous duty pay. So there I was, doing twice the work, PLUS going outside the wire—while being paid only a quarter of what he was. Hmm . . .

Why Fobbits may be mocked for never leaving the comforts of home . . .

♂

The purpose of this section is to recognize the Fobbit. According to Wikipedia, the word Fobbit is a combination of the acronym FOB and the term Hobbit from Tolkien's *The Lord of the Rings* series. Hobbits never leave the Shire; Fobbits never leave the FOB. However, I'm convinced that the infantry, the scouts, the military police (MPs), and those performing all the other combat-based jobs in the Army are merely jealous of Fobbits.

The Fobbit's deployment is usually easier to stand because he gets hot chow every day—he's never outside the FOB when chow is being served—so he doesn't have to eat those nasty Meals, Ready to Eat (MREs). He also doesn't get as dirty, because he's not "outside the wire" rolling around on the ground doing combat operations.

Instead, Fobbits are the guys running your computer systems, preparing your chow, and maintaining the generators, so you can have power when you return. They're the mechanics fixing the vehicle you broke yesterday; the communications guy fixing the radio you fried last week; the laundry workers washing your nasty drawers; the tactical operations staff making sure you have the proper assets

Paul on a mission near the ruins of Babylon.

to complete your mission—the list goes on and on. Without these individuals, the combat arms guys couldn't do their jobs.

I am personally trying to get rid of the demeaning term "Fobbit" that military personnel use to refer to them. It suggests they don't appreciate all the hard work these workers do for them, that they would rather everyone be a gun bunny (a combat arms soldier), blowing stuff up and causing mayhem. That would not work well though, because when they returned to the base, they would have that much more work to do before they could lie down and relax before the next mission.

Although, to be honest, there usually isn't that much lying down before the next mission, anyway—it's usually just go, go, go.

♀

OK, Paul's right: we should get rid of the term Fobbit. It's demeaning to those who support combat soldiers, or combat-support soldiers like myself (MPs lead the way!). During my first deployment, I might have made a derogatory remark or two about Fobbits. But after I stopped getting paid, went without chow for a couple of days, never received a letter from my family, and walked around in the same pair of drawers for a week, I quickly learned the error of my ways.

Why "quid pro quo" will be an accepted form of exchange . . .

Unless you're a gambler—and, by the way, gambling is not supposed to happen downrange in any way, shape, or form—you don't get anything you need or want, whether it's work-related or not, unless someone owes you something.

Back in the states, if you're in charge of the supply shop, people don't value you much. But once you're in the sandbox, everything changes. Who can get just about anything you need? Yep: the supply guy. He can order almost anything—paper, pencils, knives, water, equipment—depending only on the budget. So, obviously, your first task is to make him your dear friend. The next time he needs help unloading the connex full of new supplies, you might want to think twice about not helping him out. . . .

The same is true about your communications guy. Who do you think controls the internet? Who can get you extra radios? Who can get a cool-guy holster for your radio along with a cool-guy headset, so you'll look even more badass? Yep, it's the communications ("commo") guy. Who do you think sets up your computer log-in accounts, and helps get your certifications in order so you can accomplish your required work in a timely fashion? Yep, you're correct again: the commo dude. When you come back from a mission and your radios acted weird, the screens on your display systems went haywire, who are you gonna go to for help? Yep, we know the answer. So, the next time this guy needs help dragging a new, heavy-as-crap satellite to the top of the building, you might want to reconsider telling him you might be able to come by later to help, after you finish watching that movie you left paused while you went out on mission.

Don't think your cooks have an easy job, either. These guys wake up super early to start breakfast and stay up super late to clean up.

While the food may not be the best, you can't blame them—they can only work with what they get. Trust me, no matter how bad things get out front, they'll have some extra goodies stashed away in the back for their close friends—the stuff they couldn't put out during the day because there wasn't enough for the whole unit. Maybe sometime in the future (say, the 4th of July) you might want to get a steak, under the table, to cook on the grill—the one that you got from the supply guy in another under-the-table agreement. Or maybe all you'll be looking for is a few extra cookies at the end of the day. Helping this guy throw all the ice into the big, freezing connex next time might pay off in the long run.

That's not to leave out the combat-arms guys, either. The Fobbits should help ya'll out when you get back from a mission, whether it's giving you a hand with refueling the truck or whatever else they can do. Because, after all, a Fobbit is a Fobbit—he isn't going anywhere. But as a soldier out on a mission, you may find yourself on some patrol base in the middle of nowhere that few people know about—but it may have a post exchange (PX) that just so happens to have exactly what the Fobbit wants. If you want some supplies from the big PX at the FOB that the Fobbit can visit any day, you might want to think about helping the Fobbit out by scouting for what he wants at that isolated Contingency Operating Base (COB) PX. But what if last night the Fobbit said, "Sure, I'll help you out," then didn't help you park your vehicle? Then maybe when you've been to that local Army and Air Force Exchange Service (AAFES) PX at that isolated COB, it'll just be, "Oops, I forgot," or "Man, they were all out; sorry, maybe next time."

All in all, it's a good idea to lend a helping hand wherever you can, because somewhere down the road you're going to need a favor. At that point when you ask, your request can be met with two replies: "Hell, NO!" or "Sure, man; need anything else?"

I can tell you that 3rd platoon of Apache 1-10 Cavalry got what they needed from me because they made my life easier as the guy in charge of the communications shop. They were the one group I could count on when I needed to do a changeover of any sort, unload a connex, or take equipment out or install equipment in trucks. That made me grateful. So, when they needed equipment, it wasn't a matter of, "Let me check whether I have enough for everyone else."

I don't know whether they still get that treatment now. What I do know is, a quid pro quo can get damn near anything accomplished.

Why you might get caught openly socializing with the French . . .

♀

Ah, yes, our North Atlantic Treaty Organization (NATO) allies: the Coalition of the Willing, the battle buddies of the United States of America. They're something, aren't they? These are the countries that are actively fighting the war on terror with us, shoulder to shoulder (or Shona ba Shona). Their soldiers are in the trenches with us, sacrificing their lives and serving their countries honorably.

Then there are the OTHER countries, whose definition of "fighting" the war on terror consists of them standing guard outside the DFACs on base. They do a good job of it, too, because one day during my first deployment I wasn't allowed inside because I had forgotten my identification card. This particular NATO ally, being the disciplined warrior he was, wasn't going to be fooled by me. Oh no, it didn't matter that I clearly had an American accent, was of African-American descent, was wearing the uniform of the U.S. armed forces, and was armed with a 9mm pistol. For all he knew, the insurgents had flown me in as part of a complex attack directed against that base. I love interacting with service members from other countries. I've served two tours in Germany and one in South Korea. I love exchanging ideas and learning about cultures different from my own.

And, most importantly, I love exchanging MREs. Did you know that one MRE for a British soldier consists of 4,000 calories? For just one meal! Hello, Big Ben! Some countries' MREs contain wine or liquor. (Of course, I have never possessed, consumed, or purchased any alcoholic beverage downrange, because that's prohibited by General Order #1.) They also come with some of the best chocolate on the planet!

So, rest assured, fellow American citizens, we are not alone in this fight!

Paul and Kristina practicing their cultural awareness and being social with our counterparts.

Why your knowledge of Charades may aid you in communicating with local allies and people . . .

Say you're back in the States, over at a friend's house for the evening. Someone just popped some popcorn, you're on your second alcoholic beverage, and laughter fills the air. You watch your middle-aged male friend's sad attempt to act out the movie *Striptease*. He wiggles his bottom as he attempts to "drop it like it's hot" on an imaginary pole in his living room. He then rolls around on the ground in what you assume is intended to be a seductive manner. That's right, its couples' game night, and the game is everyone's favorite: Charades. You're having the time of your life as you laugh hysterically at your friend. What a great game!

Fast-forward a few months. Now you're downrange, and it's a blissful 105 degrees in the shade. And you are absolutely sick of Charades. Your unit has just one interpreter. He's doing his best, but there's no way he can be everywhere all the time.

At first you tried communicating with the locals in their native tongue, frantically fumbling through your pocket language guide.

However, you soon realized that your version of their language was a cross between gibberish and a new language you created. This new language consisted of you pronouncing their language the way your American/English mind tells you it should be pronounced. You realized it was getting you nowhere fast.

So you decided to try your hand at *Pictionary*. What a brilliant idea! Except that you failed art class in school because all you could draw were stick figures and smiley faces.

As your final attempt at good will and diplomacy, you settled on Charades. After giving an acting performance worthy of a Razzie Award (for worst actor), the only thing you managed to accomplish in 45 minutes was amusing the local village with your hip thrusts and gyrations (which might have been offensive to some of the locals, but, hey, I was desperate), sign language, and, as a finale, Michael Jackson's moonwalk. Come on, everybody knows Michael Jackson! At that point, you realized you should have paid more attention in the "Intro to Arabic" language class you received right before you deployed. Now it was too late, and as the sun set you gave up.

Who will be able to speak English depends on which theater of operation you go to and where within that country you are. Some of the locals, including members of the local national police and army, may speak very good English. Some have even studied in other countries, such as England.

Unfortunately, I'm not immune to a tendency to totally humiliate myself while attempting to communicate. One day a soldier from the local national army came up to me. As he approached, I greeted him in the customary way, by placing one hand over my heart and saying "Salaam," the equivalent of "hi." He handed me a piece of paper, and before he could say anything I said "C . . .o . . .p . . .y." As we all know, even if the other person doesn't speak your language, if you say it loud enough and elongate each word, they'll suddenly understand. As I spoke, I nodded my head up and down as if I were asking a five-year-old child whether he had to make potty.

I was very used to them coming up to me and requesting photocopies; it was, in fact, an everyday occurrence. I looked at the paper, and as I went to make the copy he said one word: "Color." Well, we had very strict guidance not to make color copies for them without

Communicating with the Locals

*   Pay attention in the "Intro to ____" language class you're given prior to deployment.

*   Ask native speakers, such as your interpreter, the correct pronunciation of words and phrases. Then remember, practice makes perfect!

*   Don't assume you're the only one who speaks English. By now the U.S. military has been in some of these places for a while, so assuming that none of the locals has picked up any English may lead to unfortunate circumstances.

*   Provide guidance to those local nationals who attempt to learn English. And don't think you're being funny if the locals are curious about how to say, for instance, "food," but you teach them a curse word instead. When they eventually figure it out, it may not be so funny anymore.

*   Find out which dialect the local people speak, and use that. Don't assume they all speak Arabic. Don't assume they speak Dari when in fact they speak Pashtu. Remember, there's no one-size-fits-all language.

*   Buy an electronic translator that will translate the words you speak into the language you select.

speaking with our intelligence section first. But it was lunchtime, so of course both the terp (interpreter) and the intelligence section were out. And I assumed this guy was like all the other guys I'd dealt with: I figured he didn't speak English.

So, once again, in a calm, authoritative, yet motherly tone, I began to speak. "T . . .h . . .e   t . . .e . . .r . . .p   i . . .s o . . .u . . .t   t . . .o   l . . .u . . .n . . .c . . .h. N . . .o   c . . .o . . .l . . .o . . .r." Now, picture me, as I spoke those words, also acting them out. I made the talking gesture with my hand, referring to the interpreter, of course. Next I used the first two fingers on my hand upside down, wiggling my fingers to symbolize walking. I then pointed toward the door to mean that he had left. For the finale, I shook my head from side to side and rubbed my brown skin to symbolize "no color."

As is the custom in most foreign countries, he didn't interrupt me during my entire performance. He just stood there with a mystified look on his face. Then, just as I was about to begin my entire routine again from the top, he stopped me dead in my tracks. He said, "You know, I do speak English."

Even though most of the local population doesn't speak English, they'll attempt to learn so they can communicate with you. If they make the effort to attempt to learn our language, you should do your best to teach them the correct pronunciation and usage of words. I remember on my second deployment, we shared our BDOC with the local national army. Several of those guys would ask us questions and elicit our help in pronouncing English, which I was happy to do with almost all of them.

But there was one guy who just couldn't get it; in three months' time he only managed to learn four phrases. There were times I had to stop and look around to ensure I wasn't laced up in a straitjacket in a padded cell in a mental institution. Every time we spoke or someone spoke over the radio, he would say, "I hear you, this is the sit, this is the chair." Every five minutes through his four-hour shift, I heard that over and over again. "I hear you, this is the sit, this is the chair."

And that wasn't even the worst part. One evening he witnessed a heated exchange between two soldiers. After that, every time he got angry he would shout, "mother b**** (term for a female dog). Sure, it was funny at first; but we learned a valuable lesson about what not to say and do around them.

Why you'll become familiar with the term "jingle trucks" . . .

♂

They're pretty much what the term sounds like. Think of a semi-truck, but then picture that a local national from Iraq or Afghanistan has decorated it with brightly colored pictures. He's also attached bells and numerous other things to it that symbolize his family and where they come from.

These guys constitute the country's own force of rugged truck drivers. They endure everything from roadside bombs to run-ins with the local Taliban forces who are upset because they're supporting the Americans. The other thing is, even though they've been put through a strenuous background check, be aware while you're escorting them on the FOB that they may be there to collect intel on your location.

Chapter 3

The Locals: Keeping Up with the "Neighbors"

Why music playing over a loudspeaker may not indicate a party or concert . . .

♀

Its 0500 (5:00 a.m., for you civilians out there). I'm snuggled down like a bunny rabbit in my warm little hole inside my sleeping bag, with only the tip of my nose peeking out. I'm dreaming of all the wonderful things I'll do with my "deployment money." I'm seeing visions of me and my family lying on a sunny beach, without a care in the world, while we listen to the sound of waves crashing on the shore.

Suddenly I hear, "A . . . L . . . L . . . A . . . H . . ." WTH?! Little did I know, that was only the beginning. Throughout the day there would be what seemed like endless hollering over the loudspeakers off base. I learned that most of the time what I was hearing was prayer announcements from mosques. However, I was informed that sometimes the insurgents use the loudspeakers to broadcast their propaganda—I have a feeling they're not wishing good will to all men.

So I requested that we use our own loudspeakers to broadcast our own propaganda. I suggested that—on behalf of not only us, but our NATO allies as well—we play the legendary British rock band Queen's "We are the Champions." Can you believe they denied that? They said we don't even have British troops on this FOB. So I said, "OK, how about 'God Bless America'?" They also denied that, plus

Bruce Springsteen's "Born in the USA" and Lee Greenwood's "Proud to be an American." During the holidays I thought that maybe we should return the good will and play "I Saw Momma Kissing Santa Claus" in Arabic.

Boy, I tell you, there is just no pleasing some people!

Why what appears to be a riot will actually turn out to be an ethnic celebration . . .

♀

One night I witnessed a group of local people start a fire that eventually grew into a bonfire. I then saw children tie bundles of hay together, light those bundles on fire, and twirl them over their heads like teenagers with glow sticks at a rave. I haven't seen people celebrate fire so much since Tom Hanks in *Cast Away*: "Look, look what I've created."

I know our educational system in the states is not the best. However, I guarantee you I could stand outside any middle school in the country and at least one out of every ten kids could explain Newton's Law of Gravity to you. They would at least say, "Yeah, he's that guy who watched an apple fall from a tree." In essence: what goes up must come down!

Yet celebratory gunfire is still a common practice around the world in places such as the Middle East, Latin America, South Asia, and the Balkans. And every year many people are injured and killed by it. There's no way to predict where bullets fired randomly into the air will land.

Sometimes the local nationals notify Coalition Forces in advance when they're going to conduct celebratory fire; however, many times they don't. Be prepared for them to use AK-47s, handguns, even anti-aircraft weapons during these "celebratory" moments. You'll witness the rootin'-est, tootin'-est, shootin'-est Yosemite Sam-in' it up in the Middle East!

Gunfire may be used to celebrate military and/or insurgent victories; sporting events; weddings and funerals; and public holidays.

Other sorts of cultural differences will lead to additional misunderstandings. They happen less frequently now than they used to, due to improved cultural awareness training and continuous re-deployments. When I served as a battle captain for the BDOC, the local national Army would knock on our door to request photocopies of documents. But sometimes they had to knock several times before we would answer the door, because they knocked so softly we couldn't hear them. Both my soldiers and I tried on several occasions to show them the "proper" way to knock: poking their chests out, standing up straight, and pounding on the door with their fists—like real men! I remember thinking, "What wimps! These guys knock like little girls." Then one day, while I was speaking to one of the interpreters, I mentioned the local national Army knocking. He informed me that in their culture it is considered rude to knock loudly. It's considered polite to knock once and wait for someone to answer. If someone doesn't answer right away, those knocking assume the occupants are busy, so they patiently wait. Didn't I feel like a jerk! This was a clear-cut example of how we were clueless as to their culture, yet were attempting to force our culture onto them.

You'll be happy to know that I did learn from that experience. Throughout the rest of my deployment, I reminded myself that just because something is different doesn't make it wrong.

Why graffiti won't be considered cool . . .

♀

A lot of you are probably too young to remember the 1984 movie *Beat Street*. It showcased different aspects of hip-hop culture, including breakdancing and graffiti. In this context, "graffiti" means what "street artists" spray-paint on public property (buildings, train cars, etc.). Movies like *Beat Street* are credited with spreading the hip-hop movement around the world.

Well, downrange you may see individuals in brightly colored outfits, but don't expect them to breakdance on cardboard boxes. I wouldn't hold your breath waiting for them to spray-paint a mural of Tupac, either.

Tips on Cultural Awareness/Understanding

* "Hey Momma, you're looking good!" No. Respect their women! If you're a male, be mindful of the local customs when interacting with local women. In some countries, it's considered disrespectful for males to touch, engage in conversation with, or even make eye contact with local women.

* "Back that thang up!" Not all countries share our concept of personal space. Sometimes locals will get right up in your business. If they invade your personal space in a non-threatening manner, don't become hostile or defensive.

* "Get back in the kitchen, woman!" Different cultures have different gender beliefs and views. These views may be potential barriers to or challenges in communication. Ladies, in order to accomplish the mission, we may have to humble ourselves: regardless of the position we hold, we may need to take a back seat to our male counterparts. Don't worry, even though it's still a man's world in some countries, that doesn't depreciate our value in ours. I believe Margaret Thatcher said it best: "It may be the cock that crows, but it's the hen that lays the eggs."

* "Free your mind and the rest will follow!" Don't start with an attitude that says, "I know their way, but my way is better." Contact and consult the local leaders before launching any programs or making any changes that would affect the community. Seek ideas and feedback from the locals and their leaders.

* "Turn that frown upside down!" In most cultures, a smile is a symbol of happiness and joy. You'd be surprised how far you can get with a good handshake and a smile.

* "The more you know, the more you grow, and knowing is half the battle, G.I. Joe!" Take advantage of the instruction you'll receive introducing you to (insert name of country here). Instead of putting your brain on pause and sitting there in a vegged-out state, take advantage of the opportunity. You have to be there anyway, so why not learn something? Realize that it may come in handy later.

* "Don't judge a man until you've walked a mile in his sandals." Don't judge. I know this is easier said than done. We as Americans have a baseline of what we consider to be normal and socially acceptable behaviors. Our views sometimes differ from those in other countries—and that's hard.

* "Patience is a virtue." One that I don't possess! People have different concepts of time. You have to be flexible and have contingency plans in place if your timeline doesn't go according to plan.

* "Oh no, he didn't!" Gestures and body language have different meanings in different countries. Don't get offended if the locals make a gesture that we would normally deem insulting. Make allowances for cultural differences. For our part, don't chuck deuces or make the peace sign without letting them know what you mean.

* "What's up, old man?" In many cultures, elders are highly respected, revered for their knowledge and wisdom. Never disrespect an elder or a man's family.

* "Baseball is more than a game to me, it's a religion." – William J. Klem. Different cultures worship different things. Knowledge of the religion of the host nation is very important. Respect the locals' religious beliefs and be careful when handling their religious items. If in doubt about the religious significance of any material, assume it's sacred.

* If you approach situations in a humble, respectful, and friendly manner, you'll gain the confidence and trust of the local population.

However, you may end up spending some of your time spray-painting over pro-insurgent slogans and threats.

I suggest that, instead of merely spray-painting over their slogans, we show them what graffiti is all about, American style!

Why a handful of dead batteries and some cut-up Cat5 wire may be considered useful . . .

I expect most of you know what an IED is: an improvised explosive device, the munition of choice for terrorists downrange. Almost anything with wire or a charge can be useful to our friendly neighborhood terrorist, and therefore deadly. So when we had to throw away wire, it was SOP to cut it into pieces of a foot or less so it would be a huge pain in the ass to put back together. And we had to take all dead batteries to a specially designated place for proper disposal.

These terrorists are like MacGyvers who can seemingly make a bomb out of a toothpick, some chewing gum, and an empty can. So to make sure your own equipment doesn't get used against you, make sure anything that might constitute bomb-making material gets properly disposed of.

It used to be the local nationals who took the trash off U.S. facilities, and once they had it through the gate you could watch them rummaging through the bags to find whatever might be useful. I'm happy there's now a new system in place which no longer uses the locals to dispose of the garbage.

♀

Never in my life have I seen the phrase "One man's trash is another man's treasure" taken so literally. Yeesh, who knew that someone might find a use for an MRE wrapper, two dead batteries, and a used ink pen!

Why marijuana is one of the main export crops: it grows wild . . .

♂

Yes, America, it's really so, even though I know it's hard to believe. But before all of the U.S. potheads go running over to Afghanistan to enjoy the laid-back lifestyle of the locals, realize that, just because a lot of marijuana (weed, Mary Jane, gonja, whatever you want to call it) grows here, that doesn't necessarily mean they're smoking all of it. Some of it is made into rope, even clothing. Do you really want to take all that rope and clothing away from the locals, I ask you?

According to *Asia Times Online*, it's estimated that Afghanistan also produces 1,500-3,500 tons of hashish annually, an industry involving 40,000 households.

Why an eight-year-old can wander unsupervised for miles, interact with strangers, and help harvest drugs without the police being called . . .

♀

In the states, if an eight-year-old child wandered down the street unsupervised while high-fiving strangers, then ended up in a field picking flowers, both state and federal agencies would end up involved.

Yes, I'll admit that most of our children in the U.S. are spoiled compared to children from other countries. While our children are fighting over designer clothes and what someone posted about them on Facebook, other kids are putting in a full day's work.

It's not uncommon downrange to see eight- and ten-year-old boys herding their family's flock of sheep to the grazing fields, or in the fields harvesting crops—including illegal narcotics. In addition, their siblings are tagging along behind them.

Most parents in the states can't even get their kids to take out the trash!

Why you might refer to a seemingly cute kid as a little brat . . .

♀

You're out on a dismounted combat patrol, doing the meet-and-greet, or perhaps clearing some building in the neighborhood. You see a boy. Your first thought might be, "Aww, he reminds me of my son." He just stands there, although he's watching your every move. You start thinking, hey, maybe they're not all bad after all; they're just normal people who want a normal life, just like us. Then the boy comes running up to you with his little arms wide open, and your heart swells to twice its size because you're thinking this little guy wants a hug. What a momentous moment: you're bridging the gap, you're winning hearts and minds, you're making a difference, soldier! He's in front of you now, with a smile that could rival that of any Who down in Whoville and melt the heart of the Grinch himself.

You extend your arms down to him as he reaches up to you, and you lock eyes for a moment.

At that moment, time itself seems to stand still. There you are, just the two of you, a soldier and a boy. You feel as if a weight has been lifted off your shoulders . . . Wait a minute, a weight has been lifted off one of your shoulders: you realize the little brat just pulled one of the velcro patches off your uniform and is running down the street with it.

You try to drop-kick him, but he's fast. And you're afraid that if you chuck a stick at his feet to trip him, there will be a news camera somewhere that will catch you on film. So you're officially out of luck. Darn it!

If he thinks he's getting candy from this military "parade" the next time we come to town, he's mistaken.

Another reason you should remember that other countries play baseball . . .

♀

Raise your hand if you've ever been to a major league baseball game. There, I knew it. Baseball is America's pastime.

Picture it: you're in the stands. You have a hot dog in your hand. You're on the edge of your seat because it's the bottom of the 9th and the bases are loaded. It's a showdown between the pitcher and the hitter. The pitcher nods his head, looks to his left, then to his right, and releases a 90-mph fastball.

Now imagine that instead of that major league pitcher, you're watching a 10-year-old local boy. And instead of a baseball, he's heaving a rock. You're the gunner inside a military vehicle in a convoy traveling through a small village. You're waving and smiling as your military "parade" passes through. All of a sudden you hear a whooshing sound as a rock zips by, just missing your head.

You're full of anger—and admiration. You're thinking, that little brat just threw a 50-mph knuckleball at my head. Boy, he's got some arm! Yeah, keep it up, buddy—and good luck finding somebody to treat that "Little League elbow," you brat!

Why you may pass out school supplies to "fight the war on terror . . ."

♀

Hearts and minds, people, remember hearts and minds. Part of the counterinsurgency campaign involves winning over the hearts and minds of the local people before the terrorists do. One way is to give them free stuff. I know what you're thinking, because I too have had those same thoughts: if we give a kid a box of crayons today, will that really keep him from becoming a terrorist tomorrow? I don't know the answer to that.

What I can tell you is that every soldier involved with the schools initiative enjoys it. Involvement can mean anything from sorting the school supplies to handing them out to the appreciative children. I've been assigned to units that sponsored schools and received boxes of donated school supplies from the American people weekly. My soldiers were responsible for sorting those school supplies and dividing them equally among the schools. They asked me whether they could go out and help deliver the supplies to the kids. To most people, this might sound like a simple gesture; but what most people don't know is that my soldiers were asking to place themselves in harm's way just to see the looks on the children's faces when they received their supplies. Those who get to be part of these missions consider themselves lucky. You haven't lived until you've seen a 6-foot-4, 280-pound freedom fighter tear up while passing a kid a pencil.

Why a vehicle burning in the middle of a highway doesn't necessarily represent a problem . . .

♀

I read somewhere that in the U.S. the risk of a vehicle fire is greater than that of an apartment fire. The inside of an engine contains at least six flammable fluids that, if leaked onto a hot surface, can cause a fire. I once heard a fire chief say that if a vehicle catches fire, you should move at least 100 feet away to avoid injuries.

Considering all that, can someone please explain to me the following scene from one November morning? I witnessed—from a safe distance—a truck stop in the middle of the road. This, in and of itself, is not unusual downrange; sadly, it's more the norm. (See "Things You Should Know Before Driving Downrange" at the end of this chapter.) I observed three males dismount the truck and stare at the hood. Then they raised the hood and stared inside for another 10 minutes. Then they left.

I guess that 20-year-old Mazda just wasn't what it used to be! That's right, they didn't even try to push it to the side of the road—they just left it there in the middle of a highway.

A few more minutes passed by. Then a different group of males in a car stopped next to the truck. They took everything that wasn't nailed down. Then they left.

A few moments after that, two males on a motorcycle stopped. They proceeded to light the truck on fire! I suppose it was in the middle of the road, impeding the flow of traffic....

At this point, I had two thoughts. First: I've seen this done before, on television—but that was on a news channel broadcasting the Los Angeles riots. Second: Wow, these people sure have harsh penalties for traffic violations!

It didn't take long for the fire to grow larger and larger until it was out of control. Black smoke billowed out. Now I was expecting someone to come along, see the hazard, and take "appropriate" action. Sure it was early, but this was a semi-busy highway; the next two vehicles that came along would surely cordon off the area at a safe distance until the "authorities" arrived, right?

Five minutes later, three vehicles came along. OK, this should be over in no time. Wait a minute, they're not stopping! Man, they aren't even slowing down! Surely they must see the eight-foot-high flames and black smoke?!

Yes, they saw it, but they drove right past it. The oncoming and outgoing traffic drove so close to the burning vehicle I was surprised cars didn't lose their side mirrors. On this narrow stretch of highway, they fought for the right to pass the vehicle first by cutting each other off, nearly causing traffic accidents.

I guess they couldn't be inconvenienced by any potential hazard a burning vehicle might present. After all, if these people faced such harsh punishments for simple traffic violations, I'd hate to see the penalty for being late to work!

Why an uninsured, unlicensed driver, traveling in the wrong lane, can hit you, but you still end up paying for it . . .

♀

"Get your motor running! Head out on the highway! Looking for adventure and whatever comes our way." Holy cow! Man, I wasn't looking for that! WTH?! Those three guys on one motorcycle traveling on the wrong side of the road came out of nowhere!

Sound familiar? As service members, we're issued tactical driving directives for the theater of operation we're in. Those directives discourage service members from driving aggressively, impeding the flow of traffic, or littering. We're encouraged to make eye contact, smile, and engage the local nationals in a friendly manner. Also, in the event of a motor vehicle accident, we are to ensure that the local national receives a copy of the accident form so he may be overly— oops, I mean, fairly—compensated for his loss.

Prior to deploying to your theater of operation, you'll receive a briefing. I compiled a list of things you should know before you go.

Things to Know Before You Drive Downrange

* Don't be fooled by any traffic signs that may be posted. They are only there to confuse you. Also, don't assume that the local national army or police receive the same driver's training we do.

* Speed limits only apply to U.S. armed forces personnel.

* Vehicles often slam on the brakes, stop abruptly, and sit in the middle of the road.

* Children often hop rides on moving vehicles, operate motor vehicles, and sprint out into the middle of the road.

* People may choose to drive on whichever side of the road has the least amount of traffic.

* Drivers often play "bumper cars" and force each other off the road.

* Mother Nature will kill you! There are big rocks and ditches everywhere.

* Everyone other than you has the right away. Especially fuel trucks or vehicles that are piled a mile high with various items, e.g., cars with roof cargo not tied down—which may include people.

* Shoulders do not exist! Vehicles will go off-road in the vicinity of parked vehicles, buildings, large groups of people, and small children.

* You're expected to share the roadway with donkey carts, farm animals, and jingle trucks.

Part 2

How We Live

Chapter 4

Living Arrangements:
Keeping "House"

Why you may end up living in facilities that would be condemned anywhere else . . .

♂

I'm not saying that we live in buildings that are ready to collapse or have mold growing in them. I'm merely stating that most average U.S. citizens would be appalled if they had to live where we do for more than a few hours. Of course, even for us, living conditions differ widely: different places mean different conditions. Living quarters range from those at a standard patrol base to the super-FOB.

Within the overall living facility, your own living space is likely to be one of two things, depending on how many tents there are, or how many blown-out buildings the soldiers have cleared out. But in general, everything will be pretty close to you: normally you can wake up and see all four of the walls surrounding your little living space.

In my case, over at 1-10 CAV, Apache troop, we were generally huddled up in a tent, with about 10 to 12 people per tent. Usually there was no wood to build suitable walls, either. In that situation, everyone reverts to sheet walls (described in a later section). At a FOB, you're probably looking at the same conditions.

The big difference comes when you get into the world of the "chew" (CHU: containerized housing unit). If you're lucky (or your first name is "Commander"), you may even get a chew all to yourself. (I understand that someone of higher rank makes tough decisions day-to-day, but I still don't see why that means he gets to claim a whole

Just outside your tents and very close by are IDF bunkers you can run to in case of attack.

room to himself when everyone else is living two or three people to a room. I could go on a rant about how, in essence, we do the same amount of work—but let's face it, they would win.)

Super-FOBs are kind of the same thing. They'll probably still have a few tents, but most will have apartment-style chews for all, especially during this later period of the war. You'll usually have a roommate, and life in your chew will be very similar to living as a single private back in the rear. If you're really lucky, you'll get a wet chew. That's awesome because you'll have your own bathroom right inside, so if you're not a dirty person you usually won't have to worry about going into a latrine that's all messed up. Once again, wet chews are normally reserved for those of higher rank—or us mean, evil contractors who never do anything to deserve our paychecks . . .

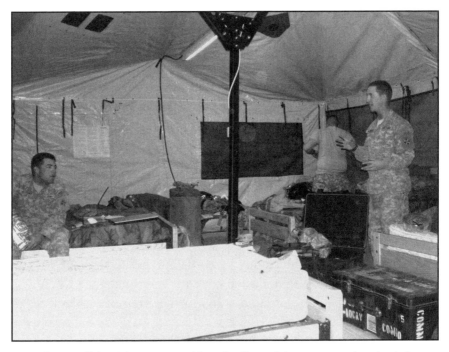

Random tent living. The guys unpacking after first arriving at our new location in Iraq.

Why 99% of your furniture will be made of 2x4s and plywood . . .

On every deployment and in every unit, you'll soon find out who the good carpenters are and who has never seen a hammer in his or her life. This set of skills really separates the men from the boys.

Who can build, from the floor up, a decent building, equipped with electrical outlets?

In contrast, who never got past helping his dad with the treehouse? These artistic fellows often become part of the talented group of people who get roped into building our tent floors, doors, tactical operation center buildings, etc. Fortunately, there always seems to be at least one person who's good at organizing these building efforts. You can earn a lot of quid-pro-quos within your group.

The downside is that you'll probably have, at best, sub-par tools and few building supplies to work with. And you still have to attend to your main responsibilities. So while you're building that nice building or new desk for the commander, keep in mind the mission you and your scout platoon have to be ready for at 0400 tomorrow.

♀

Downrange, everybody shares everything: movies, even clothing when the laundry point is backed up.

But everyone needs their own space! Back home, men have man-caves and women have the garden or the kitchen or a long walk through the park with their girlfriends.

In your tent, that little space you have blocked off with your poncho or poncho liner and sheets is your own. It's your escape from your sometimes crazy and annoying battle buddies that you're with 18 hours a day when you're not asleep. It's also the one place where you get to decide what you want to do. So much of your day is decided for you, especially for junior enlisted: what time you wake up, when you go out on mission, etc. But within the confines of your little "world," you can choose to do whatever you want—within reason, that is. I can clean my weapon, watch a movie, read a book, go to sleep, or just lie in bed naked if I want to. (Easy guys, I never did lay there naked, but you get what I'm saying.)

♀

Soldiers are so proud of their living spaces that they like to show them off to anyone who hasn't seen them yet. All newly arrived soldiers get a personal tour around the FOB veterans' quarters. Like a sad version of MTV's *Cribs*, you're greeted by each service member, who then gives you the low-down on his or her space, complete with Cristal—Afghani bottled water.

They'll show you their "libraries," which consist of a bookcase made out of a couple of 2x4s and some plywood filled with books from care packages. Then there is the "study": their computer, placed on an empty, overturned cardboard box.

Let's not forget the "bedroom," or—as one male soldier referred to it—the "love shack." Oh, yeah, I can see how any female would love to be brought back to that stained cot in the corner, complete with your sleeping bag and travel pillow. You go, player!

Why you'll make almost everything out of 550 cord . . .

♂

For your information, "550 cord" (military designation: MIL-C-5040, Type III) is a fabric cord that has a rated strength of 550 pounds and is made by multiple third parties. It's also called paracord.

People downrange need 550 cord to accomplish a myriad of tasks, including holding up sheet walls and wet towels. It's useful for jury-rigging temporary repairs to various mechanical systems.

It also goes beyond practical uses. People use it to make everything from bracelets to keychain accessories, either for their own use or to barter for cookies and the like, or to place and pay off bets. The uses of this cord are limited only by the user's imagination.

It's fairly cheap as well: you can normally buy 100 feet for a mere $10.00.

550 cord or parachute cord was originally used for parachutes during WWII but as time went on this cord became useful for many other tasks.

Practical and Entertaining Uses for 550 Cord

* Cord wrap – Use paracord to wrap items, either to strengthen or camouflage them. It can visually enhance items as well. (I bought my son a plastic sword when he was little. It was cheap and poorly constructed, but he loved it. One day when we were playing, the handle cracked in two. Being the great mother I am, I went back to the store to purchase another. But several months had gone by, and the store no longer sold them. I tried using Super Glue to piece it back together, but that didn't hold for long. I then had a bright idea: why not use 550 cord? Every high-speed soldier always has 100-mph tape and 550 cord lying around. So I wrapped the handle and tied it off. Not only did it hold the sword together, but my son loved it even more because the 550 cord provided extra cushioning.)

* Paracord bracelet – There are three basic styles. The regular bracelet contains six to ten feet of paracord, and is great for men. The slim bracelet has the inner strands pulled out, which means it's smaller, making it excellent for women and children. The loop-and-knot band is simple to make and great for everyone.

* Survival bracelet – These bracelets are different from others because the central core can be quickly pulled out, which makes it easy to pull the knots apart. It's a good way to keep paracord on hand.

* Lanyard – Use a lanyard to keep something secured when there's risk of losing it.

There are times, due to a lack of available resources, that men and women do share the same tents. However, there's some form of divider or partition between them as a barrier.

Now, back in my day (pause for the sound of my knees popping), we shared the same tent. But that was in the good old "be all you can be" era, when soldiers were soldiers. (Sorry, I've been looking for an opening to get that off my chest!)

♀

Now is a good time to address tent etiquette. Overall, remember that you're not at home, and you do live with other people. For the sake of everyone's mental and physical wellbeing, please take the following tent etiquette into consideration:

- No walking around naked.

- No hoarding of foods that spoil, or at least no opening them in the tent after they have.

- If you have smelly feet, keep your boots and tennis shoes outside.

- No night lights. If the sounds coming from PVT Snuffy's area scare you, use a flashlight.

- No excess laundry. A laundry service is free and available. If you can't get all your stuff turned in, choose wisely. If you have to make a choice between your dirty, smelly drawers and a t-shirt, choose the drawers.

- If you have an excess amount of gas built up, please be considerate of others. Either release it inside your sleeping bag or Febreze afterwards.

- Nobody thinks your pet mouse Mr. Bojangles is cute. Stop leaving piles of nuts and berries for him; his whole mouse family is setting up residence inside our tent.

- Other soldiers don't share the same work schedule as you. Your stumbling around like a bull in a china shop at 0300 is not cool. Put your high-speed soldier skills to use—practice noise and light discipline.

- Again: this is not your house, and we are not members of your family. So, #1: don't rummage through my things for something you need and think I might have. #2: stop setting your alarm clock to go off every 15 minutes for an hour. I understand your thought process; the snooze button is one of the greatest inventions of all time. However, it's not appropriate in a tent full of light sleepers.

Why you'll approach shower facilities with a mixture of eagerness and dread . . .

♂

You'll encounter every type of shower you can think of:

• The shower tent: literally a tent with some 3'x3' squares, sectioned-off with plastic, to shower in.

• Wooden buildings with metal or plastic liners inside. The shower room itself can be either open or sectioned off.

• Even better are shower trailers, which have sectioned-off showers with decent sinks and always seem to have hot water—the biggest plus.

• The ultimate is the "wet chew" referred to previously. With this option, not only do you NOT have to walk miles to the nearest shower facility, but, since you're the only one using it, it should also be the cleanest option.

The shower facilities almost everywhere provide you with a decent amount of water to shower. However, understand that in almost all places that means a two-to-five-minute shower that requires you to shut off the water while you soap up and scrub down. If you don't do this, your buddies who shower after you will get no water, and no one wants to be a bad battle buddy.

Patrol base/COP: Here there is usually a hot water issue. Even though after a rough day all you want to do is jump into a hot shower, this luxury is often not available at these smaller locations. More often than not, the water heater either breaks or just can't last through showers for everyone. At that point, maybe a third of the people get a cold shower. Even though that may be effective for getting some soap on and washing the dirt off, it really puts a damper on the day.

FOB: The same rules apply at FOB-level places: you're expected to leave after a two-to-five-minute shower. But here's a little secret: these places, for the most part, have much more water. So I sometimes get away with taking 10 minutes or more of shower time. Obviously, I wouldn't do this before making sure this particular place doesn't have any water problems.

Why you may approach latrines with even more dread . . .

These too come in many varieties, depending on the type of base you're on and where it's located:

- Patrol base/combat outpost (COP): How long the patrol base has been in existence is a major factor in what you'll have at your disposal for "disposal." In my experience, this means the "bathrooms" will be things that look like outhouses with big cooking pots sitting underneath them. There will be a hatch in the back of the outhouse to retrieve the feces pot, which gets pretty rancid and is emptied every day. But if you haven't figured it out yet, there's only one way to empty them when you live in the middle of nowhere: some poor soul has to pour diesel fuel in, take a rather long stick or 2x4 and stir the mixture, then set it on fire. The only good thing I can say about this system is that there's almost always standard toilet paper. Now, I know what you're thinking at this point: "What the hell!" But where there's no plumbing and no one coming to pick it up, that's how it has to happen. So, for the better part of your morning, people are burning off the feces produced by you and all your comrades.

- Forward Operating Base (FOB): If you're one of the lucky ones who gets sent to a FOB, the good news is I have yet to see one that doesn't have a Porta-John somewhere. They're usually cleaned out by either contracted workers or your friendly local national workers. Score one for the guys who live there, because they don't have to deal with "outhouses."

• Depending on the location of the FOB, you may even see another step up: some of the DFACs have good, old porcelain toilets with plumbing and running water—the whole kit and caboodle.

• Super-FOB or Contingency Operating Base (COB): Super-FOBs take it a step further. The very lucky people there are sometimes graced with wet chews. These living quarters, usually about 6x8, have a shower and toilet right in the room. But I'm sure you can guess that there are never enough wet chews for everyone on the base, so there's usually a very, very long waiting list to get one—unless your name is Four-Star General. The waiting list can have a few hundred people on it, and priority usually goes by how long you've been at the base, sometimes counting your previous years. So unless you're a contractor who's been overseas for the last few years or one of those unfortunate military personnel on a repeat or extended tour, putting your name on that list will likely be futile.

Why people may debate the merits of urinating in a bottle instead of using a Porta-John . . .

Some male soldiers urinate in bottles while downrange. They keep a plastic bottle beside their beds, and use them during inclement weather or in the middle of the night. Even though some females are issued the FUD, most will make their way anywhere from 30 to 200 feet to the latrine (restroom).

Or they'll try to hold it all night long. This doesn't always work out. One night during my first deployment, I didn't want to get out of bed to walk over to the latrine, which was about 50 feet from my room, in the middle of the night. I ended up holding it for approximately 10 hours. But when I woke up in the morning and stood up, I knew there was no way I was making it to the latrine.

Due to my bad judgment and just flat-out laziness, I was forced to make a split-second decision: pee on myself with my clothes on, or attempt to urinate into the empty Gatorade bottle lying next to my bed. All I can say is, thank goodness it was a wide-mouth Gatorade bottle, not a water bottle, or there would have been a mess. Now you know it's possible for a female to urinate into a Gatorade bottle while standing up!

Why you might be excited to sleep on a mattress that thousands of other bodies have slept on before you . . .

If you've never slept on the ground or a cot, you probably won't understand how this could be. But I once had to sleep on the back of a Bradley door for two weeks. When it rained, we all cuddled up on the same uncomfortable metal floor, trying to get comfortable. Just when we finally nodded off, it was time to wake up.

When you're overseas at a newly set up patrol base, you get the upgrade from metal floors to cots—but they're just a step above metal floors in comfort level. This is especially true for us tall folks who extend past the ends of the cots. Still, a cot is to be preferred over the back of a Bradley or the floor.

Past the cot level you finally get to an actual mattress. This happens when the higher-ups (at your battalion or brigade) finally send you some. But upon opening the truck or connex they arrived in, you realize they were kind enough to send you, not new mattresses, but the ones they've been using for the four previous deployments. However, you accept these wonderful gifts. You do not think about all the dirty people before you who have shared these stained, ripped, old mattresses. That's because, regardless of condition, they're better than any of your current options.

You look over the multiple stains in the mattress. You look at the dips; you know the springs are just not holding up any more. Actually, there are many ways to try to clean a dirty mattress, but most people just say screw it: they throw their sleeping bag on the mattress and hope their skin never actually touches any part of the mattress itself. The other option—the more sanitary choice, in my opinion—is to buy or have shipped to you a set of sheets, along with a nice pillow. Presto, you have something that kind of looks like your bed back home.

♀

Sleeping on a mattress is good for your mental health. I know when I return to my living quarters in the evening and I pull that sheet wall back to reveal my mattress, it does something positive for my psyche. I don't care if it is flattened to something that resembles a pancake and stained with the bodily fluids of the hundreds of soldiers who have used it before me. Just seeing that mattress makes me feel like I'm coming "home" every evening. Maybe I'm alone in that thought, but, hey, it works for me!

Why one company selling everything is not considered a monopoly . . .

♂

Personally, I think this place—the AAFES PX—is the empire of the devil. How do I know? Because, regardless of the price they demand, who can argue? I'm not saying they overcharge, because their prices, for the most part, are comparable to those in the PX back home. All I'm saying is, come on, Walmart! I know you want to come over here and have a mini Walmart right on the super-FOB—imagine the profits!

Consider giving the average American worker the ability to come over and make a good living—working at Walmart, of all places! A place where the stocker gets paid $80k a year and the baker gets $100k—can you imagine it?

Of course, I don't think AAFES would like that very much, considering Walmart would probably put them out of business. Not to mention that there's really not a whole lot of room for much of anything else.

It's a nice thought, though; it would be like a home away from home.

Why you'll consider cardboard AAFES coins as currency . . .

♂

Throughout the ages, currency has taken many forms, everything from precious commodities to coin to paper; even beads were used. However, in this day and age, the last thing you might expect when you get to the store counter would be using anything other than paper money or coin as a unit of exchange. And even those are disappearing: most of us only use credit/debit cards.

But the first time I was deployed and went to the monopolistic AAFES PX in Kuwait, I was shocked. I think I was purchasing an extension cord for the tent, because the electrical outlets were way over on the other side. The cord wasn't expensive—maybe $6.75 American. Imagine my surprise when, for my change, they handed me a piece of cardboard with a picture on one side of an American soldier doing something badass, and on the other side the numerals 2 and 5—seeming to symbolize that it was worth $0.25.

Being the newbie of the group, I was very upset. The first thought through my head was, "Wow, they must have run out of regular coin, and decided this would be sufficient. After all, they're the only game in town, so who's going to argue with them?"

Later I learned the reason for this "currency": that regular coin was too heavy and expensive to transport overseas. Since I was already the new guy in the group, my ignorance made me feel even more inexperienced.

AAFES coins. Instead of your normal legal tender expect these fashionable coins.

Why you may wait weeks for something as common as a soap dish to arrive in the PX . . .

It's the little things that matter. Sweet, buttered biscuits! How about a soap dish?

I lost my soap dish in a shower in Kandahar. When I say I "lost it," I mean I forgot it in a shower, and by the time I came back for it someone had taken it. That's just gross; who takes someone else's soap dish, with used soap in it? I guess they were equally as hard up for a soap dish.

So I was carrying my soap to and from the shower in a plastic baggie. But my baggie got a hole in it, and the soap scum started leaking into my hygiene kit.

How hard is it to get a soap dish?! Can someone tell me why there's even a space for them on the shelf when there never are any there?! Day after day, week after week I checked for a soap dish in the PX, and they never had one. I had to have someone send me one in a care package.

It's not just soap dishes. One of our sergeants waited weeks for a fold-up chair to come in. Another soldier waited weeks for a hair brush.

Now, on the opposite end, what they do have are plenty of size-6 clogs—probably in case one of our NATO allies enlists a race of Hobbits to assist us in our efforts to fight the war on terror. There's also a wide variety of movies and television series no one wants to watch. And there's an abundance of swimsuit calendars taking up all the space on the magazine rack—but no one seems to complain about those issues.

In fairness, AAFES facilities downrange are given allotments of certain items, iPods for instance. And if there's something you want that a particular facility doesn't have, you can request it through management. However, there's no guarantee it will be ordered or ever arrive, much less in a timely manner.

Why it's OK for soldiers to be hoarders . . .

I expect that almost everybody in America has seen the TV show *Hoarders*, or at least heard people talking about it. It features people who can't seem to let things go, so they end up with massive collections of stuff from clothes to chickens.

Well, soldiers are not immune to this condition. Some compile massive collections of empty water bottles, or books from care packages they'll probably never read. Maybe it's snacks brought back from the DFAC. There's a wide variety of possibilities.

However, sometimes these individuals prove useful. For example, take one of those crazy Friday nights when a group of you gather around a laptop to watch the newest black market movie you picked up at your local bazaar. You pool your snacks, but most are provided by "Fat Jim." Yes, Fat Jim may be the overweight, 35-year-old Army Reserve specialist from Illinois who lives in the back of your tent. But thanks to Fat Jim, your group has been supplied with dozens of snack-size bags of potato chips he acquired from the DFAC over the course of the past week.

The problem is, except when hoarders are producing salty snacks on demand, you want to kick their butts! They leave piles of dirty laundry that spill all over the floor, including into your area; it looks like the carnage left by a tornado. Daily you end up kicking and tripping over the dozens of empty water bottles they've saved. There are unsteady stacks of books from care packages. There are empty bags of potato chips, Pop Tarts, and energy bar wrappers scattered under their beds; this mess also has a way of spilling over into the hallway of the tent. And there's a stale, damp, moldy funk emanating from their area that fills the entire tent. You tried to Febreze it but have given up, so you just leave the tent flap open every morning when you leave.

And you wonder: if this is how they keep their 5'x5' living spaces, what do their houses look like?

Why a female may bring five bags or more for one trip . . .

♀

Yes, this one is kind of sexist—but guys, you know what I'm talking about. I myself have been guilty as charged when it comes to bringing way too many outfits for a single trip. But having deployed both as an individual augmentee and as part of an organizational element, all I can say about some other females is—wow!

On my first deployment, I traveled with only myself and my MWD. I had two duffle bags and three bags of dog food. I was able to get away with this because my chain of command informed me they did not have an applicable packing list. They said, you're an NCO, figure it out, Sarge! So I just used my common sense and threw some stuff into a few bags.

However, when you deploy with a brigade element with a brigade-sized packing list, it's a whole different story. Just for gloves, you'll be required to have: combat gloves; trigger finger mittens, with inserts; black, cold-weather gloves; and extreme cold weather gloves. You need gloves for your gloves! If you wear glasses, it sucks to be you, because you'll have to bring every piece of eyewear known to man, including: your two pairs of eyeglasses; two pairs of ballistic eye protection, with inserts; two pairs of pro mask inserts; a set of ESS/Bolle goggles and/or one set of sun/wind/dust goggles. Holy cow, I don't PCS (permanent change of station) with this much gear!

To be fair, it is quite possible you'll use all 112 items listed. However, most soldiers end up with at least one duffle bag full of excess gear that remains untouched for the entire deployment. I think what upset me most was that I was having trouble finding room for my DVD player, DVDs, pillow, and sheets. The last straw for me came when I couldn't find room for my University of Iowa throw (Hawkeyes rule!). Crap, now what am I going to do?

Why everything you own will be in a container . . .

♀

Sand gets into everything. Did you hear me? EVERYTHING! If I could find a way to wrap myself in a stealthy manner, I would. I'd put two or three layers of plastic wrap around my whole body, except that I'd probably suffocate myself. I've had sand in places I'm too decent to mention. Every day my face was covered with a thin layer of sandy, dirty filth, because every time I went outside for anything, no matter how long, I was smacked in the face with it. There were days I was unsure whether I was in Iraq or the Wild West, what with all the tumbleweeds and dust devils everywhere.

Sand and dirt WILL find a way to get inside your living quarters. I've had both my window and my door closed (yes, in Iraq I was spoiled), and it didn't help.

So, trying to keep your living area clean is a real challenge, no matter how many times a day you dust or sweep the inside. One time I had dusted everything in my room, including the stuffed animal that held a picture of my son, and swept the floor as well. Six hours later I came back from a mission, and there was sand everywhere.

How to Protect Your Electronics Downrange

* Purchase a quality case for your device prior to deploying. Cheap cases may not seal perfectly, making it easier for sand and other debris to penetrate and damage the device. The case should be tough enough to protect your gadget from extreme conditions, i.e., accidental falls, mission-related mishaps, or rough terrain. It should also be airtight to withstand changing weather conditions, chemical-resistant, corrosion-proof, and lightweight.

* Even if you have a bag, sand can still get in and destroy your device. For extra protection, put your gadget in a sealed Ziploc bag or garbage bag, then store it in the carrying case or additional container. That way, if sand does get into the device's bag, there's still an extra layer of protection.

* Don't leave your gadget in a closed vehicle, where temperatures can quickly fluctuate between freezing and sweltering. Avoid leaving the device in direct sunlight, which can damage the plastic and LCD screens. Prolonged exposure to the sun can activate LCD screen pixels, which will make the screen appear dark. If that happens, stop using the device and let it sit someplace cool and dark overnight—this should allow the pixels to reset to normal.

* Use care when operating your device during a windy day. Sandstorms blow sand around!

* Any gadget with an open port, such as a headphone jack or DVD drive, is vulnerable, so close the port flaps to keep sand out. Many plug-in components, such as wireless modems, memory sticks, and computer cables, come with protective caps to keep out sand, dirt, humidity, and salt when they're not in use; use them.

* Allow devices to reach room temperature before using them again; bringing warm gadgets into an air-conditioned room can create condensation.

Because it's so sandy and dirty, you need containers for your containers. I learned this lesson the hard way. I had a rather expensive portable DVD player that had been given to me prior to my deployment. I kept it inside the case that came with it. But so much sand and dust got into it that by the time my tour was over it was useless.

What To Do If Sand Gets Into Your Electronics

* Do NOT turn it on to test it before you clean it! Only when you think you've gotten it clean should you turn it on.

* Use a blower, lens cloth, or brush to try to eliminate any visible sand. Make sure you do this very gently and carefully.

* You can try using your own breath or some other form of compressed air to get the sand out of the cracks. But be careful: while some people believe using compressed air is an easy, effective way to clean devices, others believe the compressed air just drives sand and other debris further into the device and lodges it there.

* If it's an expensive device and you're not sure what you're doing, it's probably best not to mess around with it; get it professionally cleaned. However, downrange you won't find an electronics repair shop on every corner. The next best thing is to ask one of your electronically inclined battle buddies to take a look at it for you.

I know what you're thinking: why not just claim it on your insurance, and get another one when you get back? Well, what a coincidence: my insurance company covers all kinds of damage—except for damage to electronics caused by sand in forward areas!

♂

I'm convinced there is an evil sand demon that lurks just outside your little living area, just waiting for you to leave your clothing or other gear out when you go on mission or to your guard shift. The sand demon spends its spare time contemplating the best tactical method to undermine your cleaning habits.

Say I've just had the delightful opportunity to clean. The method doesn't matter: sweep, vacuum, or mop. Now I have a nice, clean, innocent floor.

I swear that within an hour, the demon horde will have invaded and destroyed all my work. There is no defense against the evil sand demon of the underworld. Nothing defeats the savage beast's unsightly reign.

Why the sound of rain may keep you awake . . .

♀

Ah, gently falling rain, or the sounds of a thunderstorm. One of Mother Nature's greatest gifts, right? Like one of those relaxing CDs that might cost you twenty bucks, right? Back home I love a good thunderstorm: I'll keep the windows open so I can smell the rain on the pavement, and I slowly fall asleep to the gentle sound—drip, drop, drip, drop.

Downrange, on the other hand, a rainstorm is one of the creepiest experiences I've ever had. When the rain begins—I believe "sprinkling" would be the correct term—I always wake up. This is because even sprinkles landing on a tent sound like a wild animal attempting to claw its way in. When the sprinkling is followed by harder and harder rain, the noise progresses from someone tapping a pen on a notebook to a drummer in a marching band, then to all-out applause from a large audience.

Even if I could somehow get used to the sound, horrific thoughts would still run rampant through my mind: images of the monsoon-like rain causing a flash flood and washing away everything I own. Of course, we all know that when we have rain we also get thunder and lightning. Great, the only thing that stands between me and a bolt of lightning is a thin layer of plastic—and a prayer.

As you can imagine, I didn't get a lot of sleep during the rainy season—which gives me an opportunity now to thank all the people who sent me coffee in care packages. Thank you!

Things to consider for the rainy season:

1. If you're at a newly established FOB/patrol base or your unit is in charge of building up that FOB, don't forget about the rainy season. I've been to FOBs that have been there for years, yet every time the rainy season comes there's flooding. Sometimes this can't be helped because there is no higher ground available, but in many instances if you can find higher ground, use it. Building on higher ground helps the groundwater drain away from the tent instead of toward it.

I was with a unit that prided itself on FOB improvement projects. The commanders would do an assessment of their new area of responsibility and question the unit we were relieving about areas that were prone to flooding. Once they had identified those areas, they laid down additional gravel and tore the tents down one by one. Then they built wooden platforms at least two feet high and set the tents back up on them. They built wooden walkways in high-traffic areas, rebuilt culverts, built drainage ditches, and positioned cement barriers to help control the flow of water.

Not only was flooding a readiness issue for missions, but it was a morale issue as well. It's hard to focus on the mission at hand when you're outside the wire in a rainstorm wondering whether everything you own will be soaking wet when you get back to your tent.

2. If you're in a tent or structure that's not elevated off the ground, attempt to protect your things as best you can.

    Plan ahead. If you're sleeping on cots, before you leave each day place your belongings up on the cot. This is an annoyance, but by elevating your belongings you help protect them from any flooding that may occur.

    Consider building a shelving unit for your living area, either for yourself or the whole tent. Sometimes space is hard to come by, so this may take some inventiveness on your part. Try to acquire some wooden crates, or build shelves with spare wood. Pile the tent's excess baggage on top.

3. Reinforcing your tent with sandbags will help prevent flooding.

4. At a minimum, place valuable documents and electronics in your waterproof bag, plastic baggie, or garbage bags.

5. Attempt to locate and repair any leaks in your tent as soon as possible.

6. Ensure everyone keeps tent flaps closed, and preferably zipped, to help keep water out.

7. Ensure your rain gear is accessible and take it with you on missions! It always amazes me how many soldiers either never bring, never unpack, or mail home all or some of their wet/cold weather gear. Even more shocking to me are soldiers who have the gear but are too proud to put it on. I've said the following quite often: "I'm fortunate enough to have been given two things: the good Lord gave me common sense, and Uncle Sam issued me cold/wet weather gear. I'm going to use both of them!"

8. Don't forget about your vehicles. Ensure all openings (doors/windows) are closed before you park them online after missions.

9. Remember to perform proper weapon maintenance. If you get caught in the rain, wipe your weapon down to prevent rust.

10. If you're a light sleeper, keep your ear plugs handy during thunderstorms. (Make sure to ask a buddy to wake you up so you won't sleep through your alarm.)

Why the collection of concrete T-walls throughout the country rival the Great Wall of China . . .

♂

T-walls (more formally, Bremer walls) are exactly what they sound like: large, T-shaped wall sections. They're 12 feet tall and made of steel-reinforced concrete. They provide the safest solution to the need for perimeter security, and are used to surround and protect U.S. bases and their contents. They provide protection against everything from small arms rounds to IDF. The rumor mill says each of these massive structures costs around $600, together costing the military millions. But they ensure our soldiers' safety, and have saved untold numbers of lives during the harsh fighting seasons.

Even if you've never been deployed, just think about how many bases the United States has overseas. Then mentally add up the number of these walls that surround every tent, gym, PX—nearly every building, in addition to the base itself. This makes people wonder: How long a wall could we make if we put all of them together?

T-Wall Art. Although not all T-walls are painted, the artists that get their chance sometimes put many man hours into their creations. *http://briannomi.wordpress. com/2009/09/13/t-wall-art/*

T-walls are even considered art in places like the super-FOBs in Kuwait. Many soldiers have adorned them with their unit's mark to symbolize their transition into country. Others have simply turned them into eye candy, portraying views of back home ranging from sprawling beaches to fields of green grass.

Random wall. Surrounding every area of importance, these massive walls protect against everything from bullets to IDF.

Chapter 5

Hygiene: Keeping
Ourselves Healthy

Why your whole body may have a nervous breakdown . . .

♀

Imagine, if you will, your whole body—from the soles of your feet to the hair on the top of your head—suddenly rising up against you. What if your skeletal, muscular, circulatory, nervous, and digestive systems suddenly waged an all-out war against you? What would that look like? I will now give you a brief overview, from head to toe. Warning: the following could be considered graphic—it's not for the faint of heart.

- If you end your tour of duty with all the hair you started with, consider yourself lucky. The water you wash your hair with is labeled for external uses only, with a further warning about the dangers of drinking it. Also, since there is absolutely zero moisture in the air, your hair may fall out in clumps all on its own, or when you comb it.

- If you've seen a winter or two in your day (a shout-out to all those 50-year-old Reserve Specialists), what hair you have left has probably turned to senior-citizen gray. Is it winter already? With the volume of flakes falling from your head, you would've thought Old Saint Nick was about to come barreling down the chimney at any moment.

- If you have acne and thought your face couldn't get any worse—you were wrong! If, every now and again, you used to get a pimple or two, now an entire pimple village will set up residence on your face, complete with little pimple children and those fat, stubborn, old-man pimples. To compound the problem, the doc will tell you not to use any facial cleansers, because that will only make matters worse.

- How about the rest of your skin—your sweet beautiful, precious skin? It's the largest organ in your body—and now it's the leader of the war against you; the only ally you thought you could count on has switched sides. At some point, every inch of your body will itch. There's not enough lotion in the world to keep you from scratching your legs every day.

- Your bones will ache and your joints will creak like an old wooden door in some scary Hollywood movie due to all of the miles you have walked and ran. Your shoulders and lower back will be begging you for mercy from the weight of your gear (weapon, tactical vest, ammunition, etc.).

- Your digestive tract will never be the same. If the malaria pills are not upsetting your stomach, the dining facility food will. Your time spent in the Porta-John will be equally distributed between constipation and diarrhea.

- For us females, it seems nearly impossible to keep *her* happy down there.

- Feet. "Sweet Georgia Brown," feet. I was so sick of smelling feet all day, every day. Male soldiers, can you help a sister out? Some powder, some Odor-Eaters—please do something. I felt so bad for some of those guys. Even if they weren't suffering from athlete's foot, others were avoiding them because of the feet-stink that surrounded them like the dirt cloud around

Pigpen in *Peanuts*. If nothing else, please make sure I have ample time to vacate the area before you take your boots off.

•   By the end of your tour, your nervous system will be shot from lack of sleep and the constant caffeine shakes caused by excessive amounts of Rip It energy drinks and coffee.

By the end of the deployment, you've managed to defy science: magically, you've aged six years! And that's just the first deployment! Multiply that by your number of deployments, and you're on your way to the old folks' home, in a wheelchair!

The worst thing about this horrific series of events is that everyone you talk to keeps telling you it's normal. Wow, I never thought there would come a day when I'd wish to be anything other than normal!

Why you may use some water to brush your teeth, some to bathe in—and some for nothing at all . . .

♂

Every time I deploy there are little signs all over the restroom in huge, bold, underlined letters: "DO NOT BRUSH TEETH WITH WATER." It always makes me feel so good to know that about the water I'm bathing in: that I should try not to let it anywhere near my mouth. Does that apply to an open wound, too? I now truly appreciate our wonderful water systems back home—how good and easy we have it. We as Americans have no idea what horrors water can contain until we're put in a situation where the water is anything less than sanitary.

Because water is in such short supply, the military finds uses for even the gray water. What is gray water? It's basically "second-rate," second-hand water. It has either been processed to only bare-minimum sanitation standards, or it's the leftover water collected from everyone showering the night before. While it's useful for throwing down on the roads to keep the dust down, I shy away from using it for any hygiene purposes, i.e., hot water to shave with. I often take bottled water to the showers when I need to brush my teeth or shave.

Why someone may not shower for weeks . . .

♂

It's common knowledge that soldiers live a life of luxury while deployed. Ha! In fact, even though soldiers are told not to live like animals, in some situations it can't be avoided. When you set up a traffic control point (TCP) on some unknown highway out in the middle of nowhere in a country far, far away, you can expect to be there for days, searching for weapons, bomb-making material, or anything else suspicious. For some of you dirty people, whose mommies never convinced you to take a shower and otherwise stay clean, this may be a gift from God. For others, those days may be the worst of your entire lives.

I'm not even going to pretend I've done any of those missions, because—well, I was a Fobbit, through and through. But I've heard that sleeping, eating, and relieving yourself all within the confines of your vehicle sucks a lot. First off, simply eating one MRE can destroy your insides, unless you get something edible, such as tuna. But being in a situation where you have to eat MREs for breakfast, lunch, and dinner for four or five days in a row can cause your belly to revolt in a way I'd rather not explain.

I'm also convinced that the purpose of the military-issue shovel is not general digging; no, it was made for the sole purpose of burying your feces when out on mission, so you can attempt to be at least semi-sanitary. I've never used this little, two-foot, collapsible shovel to dig a trench, or anything else. When I've actually done anything like that, we've always had access to standard shovels. So, in my opinion, the little shovel should, now and forever, be called a "pungent stick."

After you return from such a mission, put all your stuff away, and get settled back in, you head to the showers—where that wonderful, big sign says "Combat showers in effect: 5-MINUTE SHOWERS." Does that apply to you? Sure it does. So, of course you do the right thing: you turn on the shower to get wet; turn off the water; soap up; and turn it back on to rinse off and enjoy about three minutes of nice, hot water. Right? Sure . . .

♀

Unfortunately, I've experienced many shower issues. I've been through everything from water heater issues to possible electrocution. On occasion the showers simply didn't work at all.

During cold days, taking an ice-cold shower was not a smart option, especially when the heater in the shower tent was out. We did, however, have some choices:

- Go without a shower. The decision not to shower is an individual one. However, if you make this decision repeatedly, day after day, you can expect a different decision to be made for you soon—especially during the summer months! If you stink to high heaven, you may find yourself accosted by your battle buddies, using soap and shampoo as weapons.

- Take a baby-wipe bath. A baby-wipe bath is as simple as it sounds. You stand in the shower stall or out in the open shower bay and wipe yourself down with baby wipes. At first you will feel cleaner. However, baby wipes leave a film on your skin that will start to collect dust as soon as you exit the shower facility. After a few moments—when the "Wow, my privates are clean again" feeling wears off—you'll smell an odor. Using scented baby wipes over your entire body leaves a particular smell. It's not pleasant—kind of sour—but it's better than what you smelled like before. Everyone is familiar with the baby wipe smell, so they know you made an effort.

Use your high-speed soldiering skills to adapt and overcome. Most of the time, I opted for this one instead of the baby-wipe bath. Next to every living area and scattered throughout the FOBs are large pallets of water. Soldiers bring cases of water inside their tents, work areas, and other public facilities daily. When those pallets sit outside in the sun all day long during the summer months, they don't get just warm, they get hot. During the fall or "winter" months I would grab eight bottles of water, either from outside or inside my tent, that were lukewarm, take them to a shower stall, and use them to wash myself.

I would wet my washcloth with one bottle; pour the next two bottles over myself so the soap wouldn't stick; and use the final five bottles to rinse myself off, including my hair, if needed. It worked pretty well. The first time I used this technique it was a little awkward, but by the third time I had it down to a science.

A variation of this method was to fill up one of the sinks and take a washcloth bath. I myself haven't bathed that way since my mother gave me baths when I was still under the age of 10; however, I've seen grown women completely naked, spread-eagled, with one leg propped up on the sink and one on the floor, also steadying themselves on the wall as they scrubbed their unmentionables. Watching this is both impressive and unnerving. Wow, who knew our 45-year-old operations sergeant was that limber; get it, girl! At the same time, I couldn't help but think how that was the same sink I used to brush my teeth and wash my face.

Why flip flops are an ABSOLUTE necessity while showering . . .

♀

Don't think that the mere fact that most soldiers get to shower at least once a week is lost on the modern-day soldier. Having watched the entire series *Band of Brothers* several times over, I realize how lucky we are just to have facilities available.

Now, having said that, not all soldiers are as appreciative—or considerate—as I am. Everything from large clumps of hair to unidentifiable liquids, smudges, and secretions can be found within the shower facilities. Most of those things are on the shower floors, but they can also—somehow, magically—make their way up to the shower head, walls, and curtain.

One crisp morning, I was elated to discover that not all the hot water had been used up by the time I got to the shower. The morning was off to a good start! I was humming Etta James' "At Last" while lathering up my loofah, thinking how sweet it is—when I looked to my right and saw what could only be described as a possible crime scene on the inside of the shower curtain. Throughout the rest of the deployment I made sure I inspected each shower stall before stepping into it.

A lot of shower stalls I've been in downrange have trouble draining effectively, so you may find yourself standing in a couple of inches of water while you shower. Even worse, interpreters and individuals from other countries sometimes wash their feet in the sinks in the shower tents.

Time to get serious! Infectious diseases are no joke. Athlete's foot is a contagious fungal infection and ingrown toenails seem to plague many service members downrange. The fungus that causes athlete's foot can contaminate bed linens and spread to other parts of the body. Some of the symptoms of athlete's foot are dry, itching, burning, blistering, peeling, cracking, and/or bleeding skin. Ingrown toenails can be so painful you'll have difficulty just walking. If foot issues vastly limit your range of motion or other physical abilities, you could become combat ineffective.

Take precautions. Conduct daily inspections of your feet and service them as necessary.

Why you'll debate how many ways you can wear the same pair of underwear . . .

♀

This one is for all of my combat-arms soldiers within a theater of operations. Some of them go out for weeks at a time to locations in the middle of nowhere. Those in the infantry travel extremely light, only packing true necessities: water, food, and ammunition. One soldier told me he once wore the same pair of underwear for a week straight. His buddy next to him laughed and said that most of them don't wear any underwear at all.

This led to one of the strangest but funniest debates I've ever been part of—on the subject of underwear management. The relevant factors identified over the course of this debate apply differently to each person.

Preventing Ingrown Toenails

* Do not tear off your fingernails or toenails with your teeth! Sad to say, but I have seen people do both. Sure, I was impressed by their flexibility—but it's unsanitary and can cause problems.

* Use clean nail clippers and have separate ones for your fingernails and toenails. Cut your nails when they are soft. I recommend right after you get out of the shower, either in the morning or evening.

* Keep your feet clean and dry.

* Wear footgear that fits properly. There should be at least ½-inch of room left over past your toes. Your feet shouldn't be shriveled up—like the witch's feet in *The Wizard of Oz* after Dorothy took the ruby slippers—inside your boots or shoes.

- Are you male or female?

- How long will you have to wear the same pair of underwear?

- How long will you have to go without a shower?

- What kind of operations will you be conducting? Particularly, how much will you be sweating?

- Will you have baby wipes and/or toilet paper with you?

- How many times will you go #1? #2?

- What is your definition of the word "dirty"?

For those of you who are interested, my methodology employs four variations: front/back, then turn inside out, then front/back again.

Preventing Athlete's Foot

* Keep it to yourself! Don't share footwear (boots, shoes, flip flops, unclean socks) or nail clippers.

* Protect your feet—in the shower, gym, pools, even your own tent—by wearing flip flops.

* Keep your feet dry and wash them at least once daily.

* Give 'em air! When you're in your tent, try to let your feet air out. Sleep barefoot.

* Wear issued socks and purchase cotton socks for physical training (PT). Natural fabrics such as cotton and wool draw moisture away from your feet. If your feet sweat a lot, change your socks at least twice a day.

* Have a clean pair of tennis shoes. In some gyms downrange, you're not allowed to use the equipment—or even enter—if your tennis shoes are dirty. Some soldiers (like myself) wear their boots to the gym, then change into their PT shoes when they arrive. This keeps my shoes clean and dry for indoor use. It's also a good idea to alternate pairs of tennis shoes. I recommend selecting them prior to deployment and bringing them with you, because you may not find ones you want downrange in the PX, and ordering them online can take a while.

* Alternate your boots. You should have several pairs of these, so switching them shouldn't be difficult. It boils down to: don't walk around in wet, dirty shoes or boots. The fungus that causes athlete's foot loves damp, dark places.

* Dust your feet with powder. Powder helps prevent friction between your toes and between your foot and the sock. A foot powder is best, especially one with antifungal properties.

Why you'll decide it's acceptable for other people (besides your mother) to do your laundry . . .

♀

You might be interested to know that a portion of the millions of dollars the U.S. taxpayers have expended over the past 12 years has gone to washing my underwear. It was a little daunting in the beginning—having a complete stranger from another country handling my unmentionables—but I've come to accept it. At first, I was a little upset that I didn't have easy access to clean and serviceable laundry machines to wash my own clothes. However, after not having to spend an hour or more doing my own laundry, and instead receiving it back cleaned, inventoried, and folded in nice piles, I got over it!

♂

In my case, I haven't done my own laundry in years. What can I say, I'm a little bit of a spoiled husband: the wife takes good care of me, and I'm not complaining. Before that it was my mom. She was an old-style mom who had the laundry done and the brownies ready when us kids came through the door. So, yes, I've had a good life as far as laundry goes, never even attempting to do my own until I got to the ripe old age of 20.

Then I went to basic training. For whatever reason, I couldn't convince anyone else in the barracks to do my laundry for me—I don't know why. I had to figure out how to clean my own damn clothes. I knew nothing about starch, or when I was supposed to put the softener in. I turned my ACUs into white polka-dotted art pieces. The process of doing laundry seemed to me to resemble advanced chemistry.

It was quite possibly the worst month or so of my life. I entered basic training in good shape for the physical demands, but I routinely found myself in trouble with my drill sergeant over uniform disasters. After a few of my trials and errors, my Army green socks were closer to lime green. That infuriated my drill sergeant, which resulted in a two-hour corrective training session. I found myself standing outside in the sand pit, under his close supervision, attempting to hand-wash my entire uniform collection using nothing but a bucket, soap, and clothesline made of 550 cord—meanwhile doing various push-ups and sprints as I waited for him to tell me the next step in proper cleaning procedures. All of which was completely counterproductive—but I do believe that was the point.

Suffice it to say, laundry service was a must for me to survive a whole year abroad.

Why a week's worth of clean clothes may excite you. . .

♀

After giving the laundry folks their due credit for providing me with clean, nicely-folded clothes, I do need to comment on the timeliness of the service. You are allowed to place no more than 10 items in each bag, and turn in no more than two bags at a time. The turnaround time for those two bags of laundry is three days. Therefore, the week's worth of dirty laundry that you showed up with is what you turn in while continuing to accumulate more daily. So if you don't have an opportunity to drop off laundry every single day (most soldiers don't), you'll always be behind. I only panic when I run low on underwear.

♂

Regardless of how long it takes to get the clothes back clean, at least I don't have to separate whites and colors. Who knows when to use bleach, or even regular soap? Or softener? It's such a complicated process, I swear.

Why people become deployment smokers . . .

♂

I've never understood this one, but it seems to happen often. I personally don't smoke—I think it's a disgusting habit. However, I'm not trying to tell all you avid smokers out there that it's the wrong thing to do.

Back in the states, some people can go for years with no need or desire to touch anything related to tobacco. But once they're deployed, they suddenly do. Whether it's a social thing—to just hang out with people—or a need that arises under the more stressful surroundings, I have no clue.

Sometimes it goes beyond personal reasons, though. I once had someone—I'll call him SPC Jose—try to give me a Lucky Strike. He proceeded to tell me the history behind it, how soldiers way before me had enjoyed a good, old-fashioned Lucky Strike, and how if I didn't partake it would go against everything a soldier stood for. Nonetheless, my "goody two shoes" self (as smokers always put it) declined his generous offer, time after time. I have to give Jose credit: he was very persistent and he never quit. He even taught me a little: before that I'd never known the Army actually used to support boys smoking 24/7, but apparently it's true.

I've also had people try to convince me that chewing tobacco isn't all that bad. But every time I saw someone using chew and spitting into bottles or onto the ground, I looked at that tar-like substance coming out of his mouth, and there was no way I would even consider starting.

I'm not criticizing you smokers or chewers, because in your own little way you're supporting the economy, and I support that.

Why you won't care if a dog might have rabies, but should . . .

♀

General Order #1 clearly states that adopting pets or mascots, or feeding or otherwise caring for any type of animal, domestic or wild, is prohibited. But this is a shout-out to all my fellow soldiers who may have adopted an animal downrange anyway.

Have you ever seen one of the American Society for the Prevention of Cruelty to Animals (ASPCA) commercials with the images of disheveled, abused animals just looking for someone to love them? You know the ones, the kind that make even the most hardened soul utter "Those bastards!" as he wipes a tear away while Sarah McLachlan's song fades out. Those commercials must be filmed downrange, because every dog I've seen there looks like an animal in need of rescue. Can you blame the bleeding-heart American soldier for trying to bring some joy to a poor animal's life?

I saw a dog once that made me think, "Wow, he looks like my dog"—you know, except for the mange, dirt, and Cujo-like expression.

These animals give us as much as we give them. So what if they slobber a little, drool excessively, and every now and again snap at somebody! So does the company First Sergeant, but you don't see anyone trying to put him down!

Unfortunately, we had a service member die from being bitten by an animal downrange that was infected with the rabies virus. As difficult as it is to turn a blind eye to any cute, cuddly, warm-blooded potential companion—or even any seriously disheveled animal–you must take the following precautions to protect ourselves.

- Do not adopt stray animals as pets or mascots.

- Do not approach any animal and attempt to feed or handle it. You can't always tell whether an animal has rabies; it may not look sick. You could get bitten, but even getting licked by the animal can be bad. According to the Center for Disease Control and Prevention (CDC), transmission of the rabies virus usually begins when infected saliva passes from a host to an uninfected animal or human. Not all animals with rabies are huge, drooling, growling, Cujo lookalikes.

- Wash the area with soap and water and seek medical attention if you are bitten or an animal's saliva comes in contact with your broken skin, eyes, or mouth.

Chapter 6

Chow: Keeping Ourselves Fed

Why you'll have a love-hate relationship with your DFAC . . .

Dining facilities (DFACs) come in as many different variations as bases, living quarters, and shower facilities do, but can be placed in two main categories:

1. Patrol base/COP: Your standard patrol base will usually have a company-sized element stationed there. The DFAC will normally be a tent with wooden floors. The standard tent at such a base would likely be a "general purpose (GP), large," which is about 18 feet wide, 52 feet long, and about 12 feet high at the offset ridge.

    Food is where there's a big difference between patrol bases and FOBs—being at a patrol base stinks. For the most part, you'll get the same meals day in and day out—the only exception might be special food on a holiday. Salad bars and snack sections are, for the most part, nonexistent.

    Patrol bases are usually where the crazy, bad-ass infantrymen, scouts, and the rest of the people who get the job done go to eat. Who else would be able to put up with it? Only the best.

2. FOB/super-FOB: We can cover these together because for food the only difference between the two is that a super-FOB

usually has multiple dining facilities. Each one has varying degrees of popularity, but for the most part they serve the same menu items.

The main advantage of an FOB is that it is a huge step up from a patrol base/COP. FOBs have a salad bar at all meals and a sandwich bar—score! So, when nothing on the menu seems appetizing, there's always an option that will never let you down.

FOBs also have more drink options, everything from Gatorade to juices to sodas.

Along with the regular menu items, FOBs also have two or three grills that produce items such as grilled cheese, beef or chicken kabobs, omelets, etc.

Now, before you start thinking about how awesome we must have it, you also need to take into account the quality of the food. It's not bad; in fact, it's ok. But it doesn't even compare to anything you would get at IHOP or any good steakhouse. I would even prefer Burger King's offerings to most of the items served.

Why you'll probably know what the DFAC is serving every day . . .

At the DFAC there is usually a set menu and it is usually followed religiously.

But I'm convinced that whenever they run out of something they need to cook for the evening's planned menu item, they always fall back on one option. They take some meat, cook it so it's nearly unidentifiable, then apply a fairly good sauce so it resembles something people would eat. And there you have it: "mystery meat night." Believe it or not, it usually doesn't taste too bad.

Don't even think about trying to get something new on the menu, though. Unless, that is, you want it a month or more down the road. If you suggest trying something new, the cook's response is, "Have you ever tried to order something through the Army? Even something simple, like napkins?"

According to some cooks I know, the following is equivalent to the procedure that would be required. Your three-year-old asks you for a new teddy bear. You tell him to get on the internet and find the exact color and size he'd like, then print the information out from the webpage. He types up a Form 9 (an order form) and staples the webpage printout to the back of the form. Then, of course, the request needs to be approved, so you take it to your wife for processing: this should take a few days. Wait three more weeks, then give your son his teddy bear.

Why it matters that there are an infinite number of ways chicken can be prepared . . .

♀

Prior to going downrange, I had not eaten in the DFAC every single day since I went through basic training. Who knew you could cook chicken for the evening meal every night of the week and have it actually taste good—sometimes. (Either that, or it was the Matrix telling me that what I was eating was both moist and delicious...)

The following are some of the ways the Army prepares chicken; we put an asterisk next to our favorites:

- Baked (BBQ, honey, pineapple glazed, Asian, etc.)

- Grilled*, roasted, fried, cooked in a skillet, as kabobs

- Casseroles*

- With rice, dumplings, or spaghetti

- Pies

- Chicken salad

- Sandwiches

- Soup and stews

Ode to the DFAC

In a land far, far away on a murky, cloudy, cold winter's day,
A pain struck me all at once.
I heard a rumble, a growl, a very loud ker-plunk.
I stopped and looked around.
I even took a brief moment
To turn three-sixty,
All the way 'round.
In search of subsidence my belly did cry:
"Hurry up and feed us or else we might die!"
I walked along a deserted, dusty road.
Through tunnels, over hills, through thick clouds of smoke.
I finally made it to the place they call the DFAC,
The place my belly longed for,
Just in time to get a snack.
"Stop, where do you think you're going?
Better wash those hands and shake the dust
off before you get going."
All right, ok, all I wanted was a bite.
I will obey your rules,
I won't put up a fight.
You see, I've been out on a mission,
All day in fact,
While you sat here in that chair
At the entrance to this DFAC.
Oh my, is that chili mac I smell,
While I stand here
Outside in a line where it's twenty below?
Finally, after several minutes, I make it to the front of the line.
Hot damn, it's my turn! I cry.
Yes sir, may I have some of this and some of that, please?
"Sorry, only one meat tonight, better luck next week."
No thank you, sir,
I don't like succotash.

Guess I will just take my tray and stumble
on over to the pie rack.
"Sorry, no pie tonight—the trucks never came.
They broke down,
They never left Camp No Name.
How about a muffin?
Here, take one, even two."
Banana nut? No thanks, pal,
I've had my due.
Rip It one, Rip It two, and a box of goat milk—that will do.
"Hey there, who do you think you are?
Only two drinks per customer in my AOR."
My bad, what was I thinking?
You act like you're paying for this.
Calm down, grandpa.
You'll still get your Lincoln.
I felt like leaving, just walking out.
Then I remembered, you're still hungry, no doubt.
Instead I sat down, and an ode to the DFAC I spoke.
On the back of a comment card these few words I wrote:
I'm a warrior, a defender of freedom, in fact.
Would it have killed you to bake a pie in this *** DFAC?!

Why some soldiers prefer meal replacement supplements to cooked food . . .

♂

YES! It's finally taco night: the one night I know the food will be semi-decent, so I won't have to cook God's nectar, otherwise known as ramen soup.

So here we are, going through the line, all of us washing our hands like good little boys and girls, right before we start making our selections. Everyone's excited at the prospect of something they expect to be delicious enough to actually be considered food. I get my standard two taco shells stuffed with meat, plus one of the chicken burritos.

Next we head toward the salad bar. This helps those of us who like to pretend that adding salad to the meal makes it healthier, so you can polish off that huge helping of ice cream and cookies at the end of the meal and still go back to your tent feeling good about yourself. After the salad bar comes the fruit. For me at least, this is a treasure trove of delightful edibles. Back home I normally don't go out and get strawberries, mangos, grapefruit, oranges, apples, and purple and green grapes for every meal, so this is a treat—even if I see it year round while deployed. Before sitting down you can get a two-drink maximum of whatever; for me that's usually two Snapple teas.

We hunt down a table that will seat our whole party, finally lay our plates down, and sit down and start talking. But we soon realize there's a problem—a problem that may require me to push aside my meal. Joe looks at me and says, "Hey, it looks like there's a crispy fried feather still on one of my chicken wings." Soon Andrew says, "Hey, is that a hair right on top of the burrito?" Now we're all closely inspecting our food. James soon realizes that, wow, the flies must have been extremely happy today, because two of them are just chilling dead in his pasta. At this point, I'm the only one in the group who hasn't had an issue with his meal, and I start thinking, "What's wrong with mine?" So I do a thorough inspection, but to my surprise find nothing. I happily start eating. But when I take the third bite of my taco, something just doesn't taste right. Or, actually, something doesn't feel right as I chew. So, after I swallow—which should have been before I swallow—I inspect the inside of my mouth and find a small piece of plastic there. I don't even want to know how much plastic I've already swallowed.

Everyone had already been on the point of giving up and going back to the room. After I tell them about my discovery, we make a unanimous decision to forget chow in the DFAC and enjoy the only thing that would never dream of upsetting our stomachs.

Once again, my friends, I refer to God's greatest creation: ramen soup. He invented it, mother earth blessed it with her special packet of seasoning in every bag, and they delivered it to man. It has never disappointed us on a bad chow day. As long as I have a bag on hand, I will never go hungry.

♀

Okay, we've picked on the DFAC long enough. The truth is, you just don't know what the food will be like until you get there. I've been in some that would make you think you were eating in a fine restaurant, where I could choose from steak, lobster, prime rib, or even a combination. Some locations have themed DFACs, for instance an Asian DFAC serving a variety of classic Asian dishes.

But no matter where you are, if you're fortunate enough to have a DFAC, don't forget the importance of fueling your body. When you're downrange, you need—more than ever—the energy and nutrients that food provides your body.

The Army has incorporated labels to help soldiers make smart, healthy choices. Generally you'll notice three stickers on the glass partition in front of the main dishes in the chow line:

- Go Green: high-performance foods. Premium fuel for the soldier-athlete. Fresh and flavorful, nutrient-dense. Choose frequently.

- Use Caution: moderate-performance foods. Higher in calories, lower in vitamins and minerals. Select less frequently.

- Performance Limiting: performance-limiting foods. Highest in calories, lowest in vitamins and minerals. May hinder performance, limit intake.

Why you'll be happy to pay $10.00 for a two-piece combo at KFC . . .

♀

Capitalism is alive and well downrange! Depending upon your theater of operation, you may find anything from Burger King to TGI Fridays. The prices, even for value meals, are significantly higher than in the States, and some restaurants run out of things frequently.

Kristina and 1LT Rohls outside TGI Fridays.

But after a few months of eating DFAC food all day every day, you won't care that you can't get lettuce and tomatoes on your burger. After another month, you really won't care how much it costs.

There's nothing quite like waiting in line to order a Whopper and hearing the siren for incoming rockets at the same time.

Soldiers never feel at home unless there's a McDonalds, Burger King, or the like around, so these awesome franchises brought their fine establishments overseas. There you can get some home-style hamburgers and greasy fries, all for the low, low price of $4.00 or $5.00 more than you'd pay back home. Who cares that the staff are all Indian workers who don't understand a lick of English and can't even pronounce "McMuffin"?

Sorry, unless you're at a super-FOB, you won't be seeing these lavish luxuries.

Here's a letter I'd like to send:

Dear KFC,

Your original-recipe chicken is my favorite, and there are days I'd do almost anything to take a bite out of that good, old-fashioned chicken that has grown in fame over the decades.

However, I'm DONE paying $10 for a two-piece overseas. Yes, I understand the concept of supply and demand; but don't you also set up shop overseas so you can show appreciation for America's soldiers?

Ronald McDonald helping out a soldier.

Colonel Sanders' portrait in your restaurant does inspire hope in me, and his bright, smiling face provides relief after a long day's work. But I think the Colonel would be shocked to learn the price and quality of his food at what is probably one of KFC's most visited restaurants in the world. It offers his high-quality chicken at borderline insanity prices. I can picture Colonel Sanders, along with some of our most decorated combat veterans, taking up arms! He would slash those prices, striking left and right with his trusty cane in one hand and the famous KFC bucket in the other.

Respectfully,
Paul

Why you may be truly devastated when the PX runs out of gummy bears . . .

♀

Okay, gummy bears may not be your "thing," but whatever your thing is, believe me, you'll miss it when it's not available. Much like a drug addict looking for his next fix, one day I was having gummy bear withdrawals: I had the shakes, I couldn't sleep; every waking moment I spent yearning, aching for a pack of those delicious little treats.

I finally found a spare moment and made my way to the PX to buy me some. Whistling as I eased on down the road, my head held high, shoulders back, with a Kool-Aid grin on my face, I was thinking, "I'm getting my gummy bears." As I rounded one of the three aisles at the PX, my heart sank as I saw the space where my gummy bears normally sit—it was empty. Not since 1988, when I was 10 years old and lost my first boyfriend, Timmy, to some little tramp on the playground, had I felt heartache like that. It takes weeks for them to restock those shelves, and even longer for a care package from my family to arrive.

My Kool-Aid smile turned to a sad, puppy-dog face. I was devastated. As I stood there in a comatose state, the soldiers around me couldn't figure out whether I was having a stroke or about to faint. They quickly asked me what was wrong. All I could utter was, "gummy bears." They, too, looked and saw the shelf was empty.

My whole day was ruined. I had to settle for my second-favorite candy. Dang it!

Part 3

What We Live For

Chapter 7

Entertainment: Keeping Ourselves Amused

Why you might get a kiss from a Dallas Cowboys cheerleader . . .

♀

Imagine you're an 18-year-old male from a small town, now deployed to Iraq. You're a gunner and your day is spent with you on vehicle patrol outside your FOB. You received some small-arms fire, but thankfully neither you nor anyone else was injured.

Right now you stink because you didn't get a chance to shower after returning from your mission. Your palms are sweaty and you're super-nervous. You're exhausted, but your adrenaline has you fooled into feeling like Superman. You've been standing in line and are nearly to the front. You watch other soldiers as they go through the line, not knowing quite what to do or how to act. You hear hoots and hollers, whistles and screams. All the while you hear your command sergeant major (CSM) in the background yelling, "Behave!"

Now, you're up! Suddenly you're surrounded by the most beautiful women you've ever seen in your life. They all huddle around you, and every one of them smells indescribably great. As you see a camera flash, you feel a peck on your cheek. Yeah, boy, one of the Dallas Cowboys cheerleaders just kissed you on the cheek!

That's the PG version of a story I heard from a fellow soldier. He followed it up by stating it's the reason he will forever be a Dallas Cowboys fan.

In 1941, several agencies mobilized in support of World War II. President Franklin D. Roosevelt combined those agencies into the

United Services Organization (USO). Three months after the USO was founded, Bob Hope led a group of celebrities to perform for airmen stationed at March Field in California. That was the first USO entertainment tour, and they've continued ever since.

I've had my own experiences with celebrities. My most memorable and unbelievable took place in December 2001, when I was deployed to Incirlik Air Base in Turkey in support of Operation Northern Watch. The entire cast of the movie *Ocean's Eleven* visited the air base on a USO tour. I not only shook hands with but got my photo taken with George Clooney, Julia Roberts, Matt Damon, and Brad Pitt. That was one of the greatest days of my life—I'll never forget it.

There are too many celebrities to mention who support the troops. They take time out of their busy schedules to give us memories we'll cherish for a lifetime. No matter what sport you're into or who your favorite celebrity is, the USO tours have something for everybody. They're always exciting and appreciated by service members around the globe. Thank you, USO, you're the greatest.

♂

The USO is probably the greatest soldier-supporting group I've ever known. It starts with concerts featuring many tremendously talented musicians and comedians who come overseas to entertain the American soldier. But it doesn't stop there. Every U.S. base I've ever been to has had a USO that soldiers can use as a hang-out spot, with free Wi-Fi and often various snacks. KFC's regional manager for the Ft. Carson, CO, area brings in free chicken and mashed potatoes and gravy as often as possible.

I do believe the same person even brought in a karaoke machine a few times, and convinced my battalion command sergeant major to sing "My Girl." This muscular, seven-foot-tall, bald-headed, deep-voiced gladiator had the worst, most off-pitch singing voice I've ever heard—but who in their right mind was going to make fun of a man like that?

Answer: Someone DID. Snicker, snicker—oh crap, a laugh! The CSM stopped, then looked around for a moment—to target his kill.

The guilty party, a little specialist, suddenly shrank down into the sofa he was sitting on, hoping not to be noticed. Ever so slightly, some people started to point him out. Then the CSM broke into singing again, but louder and with even more enthusiasm. Everyone breathed a huge sigh of relief. We suffered through the rest of the song, and produced thunderous applause afterwards.

By that point, the specialist who had snickered was nowhere to be found—lucky for him, because after the CSM got off the microphone, he went into full search-and-destroy mode.

Why you'll count a 60-inch TV and/or projector with some sofas and chairs as a movie theater . . .

♂

Ah, there's nothing like going to the movie theater on Friday night to see the latest release, right?

Well, when you're overseas, you're probably not going to see the latest release. While there's a remote possibility of a new movie, that's only likely to happen once in a blue moon, purely a fluke.

You're probably not going to get fresh, ambrosia butter-like popcorn. Remember the nice concession stand at the local movie theater back home? Well, here there are no selections of candy, sodas, or popcorn—buttered or unbuttered. If you have something left from the care package grandma sent last week, bring that to munch on.

The opening credits will probably be something like the Morale, Welfare, and Recreation (MWR) lady saying, "All right, quiet down now, please, we're starting the movie."

Don't even get me started on the movie theater-style chairs, because there are none.

On the other hand, the closest you'll come to having to buy a ticket will probably be the sign-in paper at the front desk.

Be sure to mark your calendar with the big football nights. If you don't know anything about football beforehand, don't worry—you will after you've spent a year overseas. Football is a main topic of conversation, especially for those whose team won the night before. If you want your military career to go smoothly, just go ahead and pick a team now. Learn everything you can about your team's quarterback, and the status of your wide receivers. If it doesn't matter to you, just pick the team your commander is rooting for, even if it's at the expense of your hometown team. Then he'll be looking to you to back him up in the heated debates that will inevitably follow.

Why service members desperate for entertainment may commit criminal acts . . .

♀

It might pain you to know that your American service members downrange are so desperate for entertainment that they are driven to commit criminal acts. No, I'm not referring to fight clubs or cock fights—this is something far more serious. Yes, we actively participate in the buying and trading of black-market movies. Once local nationals have been cleared (and found most likely not to be terrorists), they're permitted to sell merchandise on bases downrange. You can usually find at least one local vendor selling pirated DVDs for $1 to $3 apiece. Which, depending upon the country you're in, means his profit is about $5 to $15 in the local national currency.

It's not our fault, though, because the selection of movies in the PX—if you're fortunate enough to be near one—leaves something to be desired. At one point during my first deployment, if a soldier had more than two television series and more than 50 DVDs, it earned him the nickname "Mr. Video." He could open up his own Blockbuster within his tent and make a killing renting out movies.

For those of you out there inclined to be jealous that we can openly purchase these movies, don't be. Sometimes the copy quality is so ridiculously bad they aren't worth the $2 we spent on them. You're lucky if the sound quality is good enough to understand the dialogue. There may be people walking in and out of the picture, or long periods of silence. Or maybe you only get to see the portion of the movie that fits between the legs of the guy who filmed it. On the positive side, these DVDs often get better the more time goes by, because the friendly neighborhood local national may decide to download a more recent version.

Disclaimer: Of course, neither Paul nor I would ever buy or trade black-market movies. I am referring to other service members who might engage in this criminal act. I sincerely hope they come to their senses and see the error of their ways. (Just as a side note: man, oh man, was the new *Conan* movie excellent.)

Why you'll consider a week-old newspaper to be "recent" . . .

♀

What, the war in Vietnam ended?! When did that happen? Okay, that's an exaggeration, but sadly it's still somewhere near the truth.

The good ol' *Stars and Stripes* is an American newspaper for service members serving overseas, and is provided free to service members deployed to forward areas. Service members have been reading it since WWI.

However, the farther you go downrange, the less recent the newspaper gets. You will consider yourself fortunate if the publication date of the copy in your hand was only three days ago.

Why you'll notice so many subscriptions to Maxim *and* FHM . . .

♂

Porn is illegal in the military! But . . . everything borderline is perfectly fine, in the military's eyes.

According to a military.com article, allowing the sale of pornography on military bases harms military men and women by: escalating the number of violent, sexual crimes; feeding a base addiction; eroding the family as the primary building block of society; and denigrating the moral standing of our troops. I, of course, both agree and disagree wholeheartedly.

Why you'll try activities you were saving for your golden years . . .

♀

Uh oh, watch out: it's salsa night down at the MWR! Hey look, after dinner the DFAC is going to have Bingo!

Why am I fighting my battle buddies for the crossword, Sudoku, or word-find book that came in the communal care package?

Why do I have an unwavering desire to learn how to crochet? Why is it, when my battle buddy asks me to join her in a how-to-scrapbook class, I'm excited?

Why all your extra time will be spent at only two places: the MWR and the gym . . .

♂

You'll consider the gym the equivalent of your coffeehouse back home. It's where everyone gathers to talk about their day, what was for chow, how big their muscles have gotten, what the best work-out routines are, what happened to so-and-so that day, how the family is, and everything else under the sun. What else are you realistically going to do with your time, other than attempt to shape your body into what you've always envisioned it to be, whether that's an Arnold Schwarzenegger-like body or the skinny little waterboy look— however impossible actually accomplishing that may seem.

It's amazing, though, how many people get into a rhythm of going to the gym five or six days a week, yet when we go home we replace that with going to bars to pick up the ladies. Another aspect of this pandemic that amazes me is that some people—myself included— spend anywhere from $30 to $130 a month on pre-workout mixes, protein shakes, weight-loss supplements, and the like. Some of us are even aware that the human body can only absorb so much protein and vitamins, so at some point all you're paying for is really expensive urine. But in general, without all the distractions they face back in the States, deployed people seem to make healthier choices.

The MWR center is normally where you'll spend the other half of your time and is an awesome home-away-from-home offering a variety of entertainment services. It's where most of us are able to get online for our daily dose of Facebook and all the other social media services we Americans have come to know and love.

The MWR center offers brand new books—just like you'd get off the shelves at Barnes & Noble—that you can either check out or take permanently. Thank you to the organizations and individuals who donate these. I'll be the first to say that normally I don't read, but when I'm deployed, this wonderful little section of the MWR seems to have a selection of authors riveting enough to keep my mind busy.

The other services provided vary depending on where you are deployed. Most locations offer something resembling your living room at home, meaning there's a bunch of sofas grouped around a large TV showing either the big game or the newest movie available. Sometimes there are snack and beverage centers; even popcorn machines—a must for good movie times. In other MWRs, there are phones for morale calls, allowing you to save your money instead of spending it on phone cards or worse—using Space and Naval Warfare Systems Command (SPAWAR) or other evil services.

(Just a side note: if any MWR employees, past or present, are reading this—you're awesome!)

Why your Facebook page and your momma's address may be threats to national security . . .

No, I'm not talking about the "friend" request you sent to Osama Bin Laden, or your daily online rants about how corrupt our government is.

Prior to deploying downrange, all service members receive mandatory training on various topics, including social media. The briefing warns about the dangers of social media: "What you post on Facebook could have devastating effects on your unit, your forward-deployed base, and the United States of America. Even your momma could be in danger! So don't make things easy for the terrorists by posting your momma's address for all to see. You don't want to assist the insurgents with any future attacks directed against the U.S. or its NATO allies, do you? Remember that terrorists—with their very limited resources and lack of knowledge of sophisticated things like computers—rely on information from our Facebook pages to further their plans to overthrow the U.S. government!"

Well, the briefing was not entirely wasted on me or the dozens of other soldiers in attendance. It did make some valid points about inappropriate—actually, downright stupid—things other service members have posted on Facebook. Posting photos of your base, accompanied by detailed descriptions of the inner workings of your job, is probably not a good idea. Also, using the comment function on Facebook to communicate to other personnel in your unit sensitive, mission-related information (such as what time you'll leave for your mission in the morning) is not a good idea. There are also morons who post "Rest in Peace" on the Facebook pages of fallen comrades before their families have been notified. As they say, common sense is not so common anymore.

So please, assist those of us who do possess some common sense by sponsoring a service member near you. If you have a loved one in the armed forces and you monitor his or her Facebook page, don't be afraid to give them a Facebook smackdown! If you see them post something inappropriate as part of their daily posting, say something. Your message might be something to the effect of, "Hey there, freedom fighter, I don't think complaints about the lack of personnel available to pull tower guard is something you should be posting!" Thank you in advance for doing your part to defend freedom's future!

Why it will matter to you that telephone operators really exist . . .

♂

You talk to the nice operator ladies to get time on the phones out here. More time to talk to loved ones = a nice chunk of change. Don't ask why it isn't a free service for active-duty service members to keep in touch with their loved ones. Considering that this is pretty much the highlight of any soldier's day, spending $0.50 a minute to do it seems a tad ridiculous. (That may be a slight exaggeration, but it is expensive.)

♀

There's no consistency as far as telephone service goes. It all depends on where you're located and the facilities available. Some places you can call a military installation operator back in the States who'll connect you to a local number there for free. But you only get one of these morale calls a week. In other places this service isn't available, so you'll have to pay for telephone service through whatever company/country has the contract. Even when operators are available, it's difficult to connect to them, and some soldiers are unsure how to do it.

What, are you surprised? Yes, I know this is the modern age, when you can stand in the middle of any mall in America, turn in a circle, and see no fewer than five teenagers on their cell phones. I do believe my generation was the last to have grown up playing outside until the street lights came on, and knowing what a "record player" was. I'm speaking to those of us who still remember floppy discs and thought VCRs were the technology of the future. In any case, when I grew up, seeing a pay phone was not an oddity, and we knew the benefits of telephone operators.

I can't remember the last time, other than being downrange or on a military installation, that I used the services of a telephone operator. But I remembered enough that, downrange, I found myself explaining the calling procedure to a young soldier. I not only had to explain how to place the call, I also had to explain to him what an operator was. I don't know why I'm surprised; I remember one of the privates asking me how to use a pay phone. Kids these days! (See **Appendix 3C** for detailed information on phone services from downrange.)

Why the holidays can still be special—with or without 5K runs . . .

Christmas

♀

Lightly falling snowflakes; the smell of wood burning in the fireplace; families gathered around the Christmas tree, stringing popcorn; the smell of sugar cookies baking in the oven. Ah, the memories—now that's a good, old-fashioned American Christmas.

Or is it? Another sad aspect of being downrange are the holidays. Sure, your section chips in to buy a table-sized Christmas tree from the PX, and you hang up stockings inside your tents. (Of course, the males' stockings are filled with many inappropriate things, too awful to mention, because—once again—boys are just gross.) Perhaps your family sends you a stocking, mailing it at Thanksgiving to ensure you receive it in time for Christmas. It's all good.

What tops it all off is the base's celebration of the yuletide season. Christmas carols blasting out of a CD player; soldiers in their winter physical fitness uniforms with Santa Claus hats on, ready to celebrate the most joyful of holidays with—wait for it—a 5K run. WTH?! Let me get this straight: I'm away from my family; somebody placed a Snickers bar in my stocking—unwrapped so it would look like feces; okay, it was kind of funny— and the preferred way to celebrate Christmas is by running?!

Oh, well, at least there should be pie at the DFAC tonight. "God bless us, everyone!"

♂

One of my fondest memories of Christmas overseas is probably the most recent. Around the first of December, one of the other civilian contractors, Ashley, suggested a "Secret Santa" gift exchange. Everyone in the building immediately thought it was a glorious idea.

But everyone was wondering who was going to get whose name out of the hat. The day of the drawing, everyone was looking to their left and right, trying to get a clue about who would be giving them

Making Christmas Special for your Deployed Soldier

* Send wrapped Christmas presents! Aunt Sue may not have a lot of money and can only afford to buy some socks from the dollar store, but that's okay, just wrap them up and send them.

* Have everyone in the family send a Christmas card. We love, love, love mail—the more the better. Send some blank Christmas cards as well, so those deployed can send cards out to everyone, too.

* Send Christmas decorations, like those table-sized Christmas trees with mini-ornaments or door posters they can hang up. I know plenty of soldiers who loved receiving these. Their families sent the trees undecorated so the soldiers could dress them up. This gives them something to do and gets them in the holiday spirit. Maybe a Christmas stocking filled with candy, or whatever you usually fill it with at your house. Christmas lights are great to hang up inside their tent or office. (And don't forget a Santa hat!)

* Send Christmas cookies! Nuff said.

* Send CDs of Christmas/holiday music! If you can't remember or don't know what kind of music they like, just send a generic Christmas CD. Who cares whether it's Elvis or Justin Bieber singing "Silent Night"?

* Send Christmas movies! If you've never seen *A Charlie Brown Christmas*, you've lived a sheltered life and I feel sorry for you. Consider the charming tale of a boy who wants a Red Ryder BB gun for Christmas in *A Christmas Story*. I have to confess, I've never watched *It's a Wonderful Life*, even though back home they play it every two hours during the two weeks leading up to Christmas. However, if that's your family's thing, send it!

their Christmas surprise. But between the puzzled and surprised looks, no one could really tell who had drawn which name. Over the next two or three weeks, secrets were kept, although subtle hints were delivered here and there about what someone would like to receive on Christmas Day.

But there was still plenty of room for speculation. What will the prankster in the group get his person? What will the happy-go-lucky guy get his person? What will the head NCO get her person? What will the artist in the group create for his person? What will the contracting civilians get the army guys? During the weeks prior to Christmas, these questions and more fueled anticipation of the upcoming event.

When the day finally came, the gifts were so thoughtful that you could see a glimmer in each person's eyes as they opened their packages. Some got war books; one got a 550 cord wreath (which looked awesome, and in my opinion was very creative); some got fantastically fragranced soaps and shampoos; some got blankets with their favorite *Sons of Anarchy* characters on them.

After all the gifts were unwrapped, the work started again. But everyone could tell that the wrapped Christmas gifts had provided the five minutes of bliss we all needed that holiday season.

Halloween

Halloween is my favorite holiday. I used to love to go trick-or-treating as a kid. I grew up in a small town in Iowa, so we could be out all night and my mom didn't have to worry about us being kidnapped. My siblings and I would wander down street after street, going door to door. When we filled up our bags with candy, we'd make our way back home and drop them off. Our mother would give us more bags and we'd head right back out for another round.

I remember all the cool costumes we'd see as we passed kid after kid through the night. Keep in mind, this was the 80s, so you had Ripley from *Alien*; He-Man; Freddy from *Nightmare on Elm Street*; and of course, the Madonna look-a-likes—every other girl had leggings, lace fingerless gloves, and bangle bracelets.

We didn't have a lot of money growing up, but you'd be surprised at what my mom could do with a Halloween makeup kit and things from around the house. She gave us old dish soap bottles to use as squirt guns. She wrapped our hands in aluminum foil to make boxing gloves. Little did I know her inventiveness and thriftiness would come in handy later—downrange!

So now it's October in the sandbox, there's a cool breeze in the air, and Halloween is in full effect! Everywhere you go somebody is trying to scare you with a fake spider they got in a care package mailed from back home. Somebody has cut out little paper ghosts, written "Boo!" on them, and used them to decorate their office door. At the DFAC, an orange and black sign posted at the entrance says "Happy Halloween." There's a good chance that if you eat another piece of candy corn, you're going to be sick.

So here we all are, spending yet another holiday downrange—and the only thing we have to look forward to is yet another 5K run! As you may be able to tell, I've never enjoyed running. Even after all my years in the Army, I have yet to understand how the words "fun" and "run" can go together in the same sentence. But surprisingly, this one actually turned out to be kind of fun.

For this Halloween 5K, we were allowed to dress in costume. Many soldiers didn't find out about the run itself, or that they could dress in costume, until a week beforehand, so there was no way their family could mail them a costume in time.

I was able to help out a few soldiers with costume ideas. One male soldier ended up using a mop head for hair because he was supposed to be Rick James' b****. Another guy was wrapped up from head to toe in toilet paper—he was a mummy. (His limbs were wrapped individually so he could still run.) It was quite a sight, seeing everybody out there running in costume while Michael Jackson's "Thriller" blasted out of the CD player. I wonder what the local national army thought about that?

Mother's Day

Mother's Day became a recognized holiday in the United States in 1914. Yes, ladies, you would have thought they'd have gotten a clue earlier. I mean, even Adam knew better than to cross Eve—even if that did mean the Fall of Man. Every man who knows what's good for him makes sure Mother's Day is a special day, complete with the traditional breakfast in bed, with the kids helping out, of course. Ladies, you know you love those burnt pieces of toast, sour, homemade orange juice, and runny eggs—it's a tradition! (And without the little ones helping out, it's just not the same.) You expect a day free from

---

Making Mother's Day Special for a Deployed Mother

* Mail her a package. Send it several weeks ahead of time, with express instructions not to open it until Mother's Day.

* Record a video message from your family on a DVD. If you're a military family, check with your family support group (FSG) for additional information (See **Appendix 3E**). They can arrange for a pre-recorded holiday message or a video teleconference (VTC) with your soldier downrange.

* Buy the kind of card where you can record a short message to your loved one if you can't get access to a video camera or a VTC. Similar stuffed animals are available as well.

* Send her things that will make her day special. If she loves sitting in her bathrobe with her slippers or watching her favorite movie on Mother's Day, send her those things; if you always treat her to a day at the spa, send her a manicure set, a loofah, and some nice body wash.

* Send her a gift that's not so expensive, but that you know she'll like, say, chocolate or a bouquet of artificial flowers. Don't send expensive jewelry because it may get stolen, lost, or damaged.

* Have the kids draw her pictures. One subject could be what they would have made her for breakfast. Or maybe some flowers. Maybe include a recent family photo on the card. She'll love getting whatever is your "traditional" homemade Mother's Day card.

* Be sure to send her an email or post a message on Facebook on Mother's Day. Let her know that she is thought of, and that her loved ones at home are waiting for her.

* Above all, be sure to include your children in the process of putting her package together and letting her know she's loved.

---

household chores, and perhaps even a gift or flowers. It's the one day out of the year we mothers are treated like the queens we are.

So, surviving this holiday downrange is difficult. On the morning of, your kids don't come running in with smiles, and you don't get to share in a laugh as they cover you with kisses. They aren't there to present you with their makeshift Mother's Day card that has the words "I love you" spelled out in macaroni. It's natural, ladies, for our hearts to feel a little heavy on this day.

That makes it important to surround yourself with your sisters-in-arms. Spend the day celebrating yourselves! I remember on my first deployment, everybody tried really hard to make the day special for us. Outside of the main DFAC they colored the rocks with spray paint and spelled out "Happy Mother's Day." When we walked in, DFAC representatives greeted each female at the door and asked whether she was a mother. When I responded "yes," they took my tray and carried it for me, through the chow line and to my seat. They also presented me with a flower. I'll never forget the look on my escort's face when he wished me a heartfelt "Happy Mother's Day."

They also brought in a karaoke machine, and any mother could go up and sing whatever song she wanted. Several guys also went up and sang songs in honor of their mothers or wives.

That day I gave Uncle Sam a thumbs up!

Why you might ask everyone you know to send you Jack Daniels sunflower seeds . . .

♀

General Order #1 clearly states that individuals are prohibited from the introduction, possession, sale, transfer, manufacture, or consumption of any alcoholic beverage.

As a Military Police noncommissioned officer in the United States Army—one who's also seen entire seasons of the HBO series *The Wire*—I can tell you that I've seen some stuff! That includes people desperate for a mind-altering high doing desperate things. On my first deployment I was doing double duty as a PEDD handler as well as kennel master (a fancy term for the boss of all the other dog teams). I went with a narcotics detector dog team to supervise a health and welfare inspection of one of the units on base.

As we walked around from tent to tent, I noticed several jars outside one tent. Inside the jars was some rotten fruit and a liquid. The First Sergeant said, "They're making homemade hooch." I said, "Excuse me?!" He repeated himself. Still seeing a puzzled look on my face, he explained that they were making liquor. For the next half hour, the First Sergeant (who was from Kentucky) educated me on the production of moonshine.

I understand that back in the 1800s that's how alcohol was made. I also understand that slavery was still legal then! What the heck!

I admit that mine is the perspective of a person who gets "tore up" from one bottle of Boone's Farm. But for all of you alcoholics out there, I guess the matter really is that serious. So serious, in fact, that one soldier told me he was having his family send him 10 packs of sunflower seeds—the Jack Daniels kind—just so he could "have a drink" by sucking on the seeds by the mouthful. Wow!

Why you won't be considered an alcoholic even if you drink beer all day long . . .

♂

We've let you know that alcoholic beverages are not allowed downrange in any shape or form. But would you still enjoy your favorite brew if it didn't have the 5–9% alcohol content? No? Most people won't touch a non-alcoholic beer.

But apparently there really are true beer fanatics who just like the taste, and I'm not putting them down in any way. So, if you meet someone who honestly just likes the taste of their favorite beer, give 'em a high five—along with a free beer.

Of course, it'll be an O'Doul's, or something like it. They're available at your local, friendly, neighborhood PX for less than a dollar, and will surely put a smile on your friend's face. Depending on your location, the DFAC may even have several non-alcoholic beers as well—for free!

Why you may finally decide it's the time to go to college . . .

♀

You probably started off strong when you first joined. You were so excited by the idea that tuition was free to any DoD-recognized college that you signed up for as many classes as you could. This, of course, quickly burned you out, and your passion for furthering your education quickly dwindled. Month after month—or even, as in my case, year after year—you kept promising yourself you'd go back.

Now you're downrange and deployed in a war zone. You have more time on your hands than you thought you'd have. Sitting on a Porta-John one day, you get the bright idea that now would be the right time to go back to school.

If you think this scenario applies to the future you, there are a few things you should complete prior to going downrange to make the transition as easy as possible, especially if you're a first-time college student.

Tips for Attending College

* Speak with a counselor at your installation's education office.

* Request a Joint Services Transcript (JST). The JST is a computerized transcript system that produces official transcripts for those eligible who request them; it now services the Army, Navy, Marine Corps, and Coast Guard, active-duty, reserve, and veterans. The transcript lists and provides descriptions of your military education and job experiences, and offers college credit recommendations. You may find that you'll have to take fewer classes than you thought. Some colleges require that you obtain residency status, which requires you to take anywhere from three to six college credit hours before they'll evaluate your AARTS/JST transcript. Some colleges will give you more credit for classes than others will. Once again, it's a good idea to speak to the education counselor and to the colleges made available to you through the education center. Be aware that the colleges represented in most education centers on military installations are not the only colleges you can attend for free, but they are some of the most popular. For more information go to http://aarts.army.mil/ or https://jst.doded.mil.

* Go Hawkeyes!!! Sorry, that was just another plug for the great state of Iowa. However, once you've figured out which college you want to attend, stop by and see them. No, not the actual campus, unless you're close geographically. Instead, pick up the college's catalog. It contains school policies and procedures; majors offered and the curriculums to follow; required courses; course pre-requisites; course descriptions; and more. You shouldn't register for classes without reading this first.

* "I don't write so good!" Some colleges require you to take placement tests for math and English. You may need to brush up on the basics before you can even take college-level classes.

* Stuff happens! You never know what life will bring, especially when you're in the military. If you sign up for a class, then a few days later change your mind, make sure you withdraw. Unlike some things in life, you can't just ignore it and expect it to go away. If you don't, you may find yourself paying for a class you never attended. To officially withdraw, you need to go through your education portal, such as Go Army Ed, and notify your school.

* Actually study! And do your own work! I know this may be difficult for those who are familiar with CliffsNotes, but if you're found to have plagiarized or cheated, you'll receive an F. If you don't study, or you choose to cheat and receive an F, you may be required to pay for the course out of your pocket.

* Don't attempt to carry too much weight! If you get overzealous and sign up for three courses in one semester, you'll feel it. Don't attempt too many classes while fulfilling your military obligation. A lot goes into taking a college class, including study time, doing homework, research in a library or over the internet, and writing papers.

* Finally, before you go downrange, check with your local education center for a list of locations where education centers are available. The following list is not all-inclusive. It was current as of October 2012.

  - Afghanistan: Bagram, Kabul, Kandahar, Salerno

  - Africa: Djibouti

  - Kuwait: Camp Arifjan, Camp Buehring

  - Egypt: North Camp MFO, South Camp MFO

  - Qatar: Camp As-Sayliyah

Why you might try activities that will cause you to need the expertise of either a physician or poison control . . .

> **Note: The following activities have not been authorized and should not be attempted by any soldier or civilian—no matter how bored you are! Even though they are VERY entertaining for the rest of us to watch . . .**
>
> * Capturing a camel spider and . . .
>
>   - putting it in your mouth.
>
>   - putting it in your battle buddy's sleeping bag.
>
>   - throwing it at your buddy.
>
> * Capturing scorpions and making them fight.
>
> * Taking turns shooting each other with nonlethal or less-than-lethal rounds.
>
> * Throwing things into the burn pit just to watch them explode.
>
> * Jumping off the top of a bunker and attempting to do a combat roll.
>
> * Attempting to make homemade fireworks and using them to blow up things.
>
> * Daring each other to take the "milk challenge" (drinking a gallon of milk within 60 minutes without vomiting) with the milk out of the DFAC.
>
> * Seeing how many non-alcoholic beers you have to drink before you think you get a buzz—or puke.
>
> * Daring each other to drink hand sanitizer, or various other things that have the poison control hotline number right on them!
>
> * Dropping a grenade inside a vehicle—as a "prank."
>
> * Attempting to make moonshine from fuel.
>
> * Eating at a local meat stand.

Why some of your happiest days will be when packages from the civilized world arrive . . .

♂

Oh, happy day! You know the kind: a Friday night when you go out to a bar and get into a ridiculously drunken state, then talk about it with your friends on Monday. Or when you meet your college buddies at the coffeehouse on the corner to have a "study session" in advance of next week's exams. Or when you take your new girlfriend to see the newest and greatest movie that just hit the theaters. Or when your mom calls to wish you luck at that job interview that's stressing you out.

Well, guess what? Those days are gone. No more happy-go-lucky, amazing Friday nights of madness, with the freedom to do whatever your little heart desires. You're in a war zone, my friend. News flash: your new entertainment is big bombs causing explosions right next to you 24 hours a day. To mix it up a little, there may even be the occasional firefight.

You—the spouse, a brother or sister, or any patriotic civilian—can change this horrific reality with one simple card, letter, or care package filled with goodies. Five minutes is all it takes to put words on paper and mail it to a loved one or soldier. When you're at Walmart, just take a moment to ask yourself: if I were thousands of miles away from anything even remotely resembling a Walmart, what would I want?

And, trust me, it makes an amazing difference to the stressed-out soldier receiving the package or letter.

However, there are some things that are NOT appreciated: When you send a care package to a group of soldiers but you fill it with 500 female hygiene supplies when there are approximately eight females on the entire base....When you assume we are all a bunch of compulsive gamblers and send 70 decks of playing cards. Although dental floss is needed, when you send a thousand units for a unit of four thousand, please think again. All I'm saying is, we love care packages, but try to send moderate amounts, and think about the size of the place you're sending it to.

Here are some other points:

- To all my young cousins: trust me, the farting machine did indeed provide hours of entertainment.

- Wives, even though your husbands probably won't say so, the little spray of perfume and the big red lipstick kiss on the envelope are also highly appreciated—even though they're going to get us laughed at later on.

- For those of you with a little more $ to shell out, movies/series/music of any sort are always appreciated. What else do we have to do except catch up on the latest episodes of *True Blood* or *Sons of Anarchy*?

- Children of deployed soldiers, trust me when I say your mom and dad do love you tons, and your favorite teddy in the mail will likely be cuddled with and kept very close to their hearts.

♀

The morale of a soldier can change dramatically just by receiving a piece of correspondence from someone. I distinctively remember one soldier who had not received a package since he deployed. Then he received one from his grandmother, and he let out a scream. Not a yell, but a 13-year-old-girl-at-a-Justin Bieber-concert-type scream. "Cookies!" he exclaimed. He then ran to a dimly lit corner, and the only sounds we heard for the next 30 minutes were wrappers crinkling, lips smacking, and the occasional softly mumbled words, "My precious."

Why you might even look forward to hearing from those annoying in-laws . . .

♂

If you're married, you'll be emailing or sending off letters constantly. It starts with your immediate family: your wife or husband. If you have any children, you'll call and check on how school was or how the baseball game went. But probably the most interesting family members you'll talk to are the cousins and uncles—people you don't normally see for years, and may even have never talked to in your life.

Those of you who've been overseas know what I'm talking about. At some point, out of the blue, Aunt Helga will send you a letter or email saying how much she and Uncle Henry miss you and how she hopes everything is going okay. They finally figured out that someone in their family was serving overseas, and took the time to message you—even if it was nothing more than the standard "missing you" piece of mail.

But if those of you back home can do so, try to put a little extra into those letters. The soldier already knows you're thinking of him and you hope he comes home soon. Go on from there. Merely talking about your daily activities—maybe how you got a great deal on that TV you'd been eyeballing for months—will create in your loved one or friend a fond remembrance of home. It will also remind him of the reason he's there: to make sure you can go about the day-to-day business of your life uninterrupted by terrorists on domestic soil. When his lights go off at night, he'll most likely be re-reading the notes you sent him. So take great pride in knowing that you made sure his last thought before falling asleep was of home.

Why you might enjoy being someone's "pen pal" . . .

♂

I know some of you are thinking, really? But by the time you have been gone long enough to learn more than you ever wanted to know about the guys to your left and right, and they in return know nearly everything about you from childhood to the present, all you want to do is communicate with someone "normal." The definition of normal is "someone who has no idea what you're going through, and is just generally interested in your well-being."

Yes, your superiors are interested in you and your welfare. But you've already talked about everything there is to talk about with them hundreds of times. You're primed to take comfort in hearing about ordinary people's everyday issues: like being late to pick up the groceries, so dinner ended up being late, and no one got much sleep; or the piling up of bills from one week to the next. In other words, exactly what you yourself would normally think about—if you weren't in the middle of the desert worrying about your next mission, or anticipating the incoming fire that often comes around lunchtime.

Conversations with your "pen pal" can take you into that other world. You can almost picture yourself in those particular situations: you're back home, driving down the road to King Soopers or Food Lion; or you're sitting on the sofa opening the mail and finding another unexpected bill. This visualization allows you to think to yourself, "I wish my problems were that simple…."

Why you'll complain about how little money you're making, but have every intention of blowing it all in the first month you're back . . .

♀

We accomplish more before 8:00 a.m. than most people do all day. So why is it that, even with the additional benefits meant to compensate us for deploying to a theater of operation—a place where we can be killed—some soldiers wouldn't even be considered middle class?

Downrange you can hear a soldier ranting on this tangent for hours on end. Other soldiers will gather around in a circle, nodding their heads in agreement, and offering the occasional "Amen, brother." Finally, after what seems an eternity, the rants about the lack of compensation for defending freedom's future run down.

The next question is always, "So, what are you going to do with the extra dough?" I know one guy who returned home and spent more than $3,000 on booze at a bar in his hometown. It's amazing: money is the only form of compensation we're given for sacrificing years of our lives and endangering our lives daily—and we can't wait to blow it as soon as we get home. By the way, I'm taking my family on a cruise to the Caribbean. (See **Appendix 2A** regarding deployment entitlements.)

Ways to Spend Deployment Money

Responsible Ways

* Invest it.

* Start a college fund for your children.

* Start a wedding fund for your daughter(s).

* Put it in a savings account for future use.

* Pay off bills.

* Purchase additional life/medical insurance for your family.

* Buy a house, or make home repairs/improvements on existing house.

* Donate some to charity.

* Help out a family member or friend in a financial crisis.

Fun Ways

* Vegas—gambling and showgirls! Buy drinks for everybody! Take the opportunity to feel like a rich and famous person at a club. Stand on top of a table and loudly announce, "Drinks are on me!"

* Take an awesome (and much-needed) vacation.

* Purchase boy toys (boat, muscle car, motorcycle, etc.).

* Visit a gentlemen's club.

* Start knocking things off the bucket list.

* Throw an epic party.

* Spoil the family at Christmas.

* Attend the Iowa State Fair! (Shut up, Paul! It's on the top 10 list of "Things to Do in the Summer"! It's only a coincidence that I'm from Iowa!)

* Instead of attending the Iowa State Fair, take the entire family to Aspen, Colorado, for a ski trip. (Paul strikes again!)

♂

Here's an example of what we're talking about. I'll give this soldier the code name "Private Mustang." The code name explains a lot. With almost every paycheck, this single guy would talk about whichever new part he was going to buy for his sweet 1960s Mustang. He claimed he was "soupin' it up," but this guy had almost no mechanical skills. So he had the parts sent to his parents—I think in Washington State—but his car was sitting in a storage facility in Colorado Springs, where our unit is based.

There are a couple of kickers to this story. Since he had no idea how to install all these parts, he was probably going to try to con someone into helping him; but if he couldn't, he was going to have to hire someone. And not only was he paying to ship all the parts to his parents, he would have to ship them all back to Colorado when he returned.

Some people would routinely buy clothing online and have the clothes sent home for them to wear when they went on mid-tour leave or when they got home for good. I never understood this. What if the clothes didn't fit? By the time you got home, it would be too late to return them.

I understand splurging every so often, but the people who received the most laughs were those who went home on mid-tour leave and came back broke, with their savings account emptied out. They would say how they had helped out their brother, sister, mom, uncle, cousin, or whoever. Now, this might sound horrible, but I think your family would understand if you kept a little of that money for yourself, since you earned it by taking "Incoming!" pop shots and everything else over the course of the year.

Why you'll consider it acceptable to know so much about Chuck Norris . . .

♀

I want you to know that I was a Chuck Norris fan way before it was cool to be a Chuck Norris fan (i.e., *Firewalker*). I even own up to watching *Walker, Texas Ranger* on occasion.

The Chuck Norris phenomenon has traveled around the world, including downrange. It's so common that one of my commanders, while he was traveling back to our base in a convoy, asked me to send him the Chuck Norris joke of the day. The Chuck Norris joke of the day is also included in many commander's update briefs as a way to wrap up the long, tedious, seemingly endless power point presentations. I think it's their way of getting everybody to stay until the end of the briefing rather than making up an excuse to ditch.

By the way, today's Chuck Norris Thought for the Day is: Every dinosaur skull ever found has had the imprint of a size-15 cowboy boot in its jaw. Scientists are baffled—but we know damn well why.

Why you'll be able to relate to the movie Limitless *. . .*

♀

Limitless revolves around the concept that humans only access 20% of their brains. The idea is that our brains are big libraries of knowledge, and all we're missing is a card catalog or file menu to tell us where to find the information we need. If you have even seen *The Matrix*, Neo (Keanu Reeves) had a needle shoved into his brain and suddenly knew karate? A very cool concept indeed.

Having seen both movies, I realize we already have those powers, but just don't realize it. Have you ever been sitting on guard duty, traveling in a convoy, or just walking around the FOB and had a random thought? You didn't know why you were thinking about it, or where the thought came from. For example, one time I was walking to the DFAC for breakfast. The morning was glorious: the sun was rising and there was a crisp breeze in the air. I'd gotten a full night's rest. So I was feeling good, like a disciplined warrior should. Then, all of a sudden—it happened. Similar to John Travolta getting hit by that flash of light in *Phenomenon*, there I was humming "Moon River." WTH?! Where did that come from? How do I even know that song? What movie have I ever watched that has that song in it? Oh well, who cares; it's a catchy tune.

One hour later, I was walking to work—and it happened again. "I'm Henery the Eighth I am, Henery the Eighth I am, I am! I got married to the widow next door; she's been married seven times before." Now, wait a minute, I know this . . . *Dirty Dancing*? No. *Sister Act*? No. *Ghost*? Yes, that's it—*Ghost*! Wow, when was the last time I saw that movie?

Why philosophical debates can account for hours of your day . . .

What would you think if someone told you that educated, disciplined warriors from the most highly trained, best-equipped armed forces in the world engage in philosophical debates that last for hours? You might think, wow, I'd like to be a fly on that wall. I wonder, do they discuss world peace? Military strategy? Politics? Maybe they debate for hours over which candidate they will support for the U.S. presidency.

You might think so but when soldiers are in a theater of operation, those are the last things they tend to talk about. Instead, I was once asked, "What do you think would happen if a zombie bit a werewolf? Would the werewolf turn into a zombie? Or, what if a zombie bit a vampire? Technically, a vampire is already a member of the undead, like zombies. So, what would happen to the vampire?" The zombie debate led into another that lasted for hours: what would happen if zombies took over the earth?

At a moment like that, you realize how little you really know about the people standing to your left and right. Who knew Sergeant Jones was a survivalist and has weapons, ammunition, water, and food, all stockpiled in a bunker on his property? So when zombies take over the earth, he'll be prepared. Notice that I said "when"—because that's the word he used.

♂

The first thing to point out is that you'll have a lot of time on your hands. I don't want other soldiers and retirees out there getting the idea that we just sit around and do nothing. I'm merely stating a fact to note that there will be times when you will be on guard duty for hours with your buddy and there won't be much to do, other than talk. After talking about home and what you're going to do when you get back, the conversation sometimes leads toward bigger questions, i.e., life, politics, religion.

For example, I stood tower guard with SPC Bradferd at Um Quasar patrol base. This was an eight-hour guard shift, about nine months into the deployment. We must have talked about everything concerning religion, from the different types to why he didn't believe in one over the other. How my dad is a chaplain in the Navy and I grew up in the Lutheran faith. How growing up in different areas made people the way they were in relation to religion.

Just random thoughts from two bored soldiers. That conversation alone probably could have filled up a whole book.

Why so many people find God . . .

♀

Here's a quote from one of the greatest movies of our time, *Forrest Gump*:

"Have you found Jesus yet, Gump?"

"I didn't know I was supposed to be looking for him, sir."

Why does it take people getting shot at, blown up, and rocketed for them to realize how precious life is? Why didn't we take the hint after watching the first *Final Destination*: that every day is a gift, and we can die at any moment?

Before we leave for deployment, every soldier must get his/her affairs in order, including executing a will. Most of us sign up for additional life insurance. But it's not until "stuff gets real" that we start finding religion. There's a saying about downrange: that you'll either become an alcoholic or find God. Well, I never lost Him— but I did reintroduce myself a couple of times, just to make sure He remembered me.

As with many other things, your location will dictate the level of ministry services available to you.

- It may simply consist of your unit's chaplain and a group of soldiers, sitting on a pile of rocks, huddled in a cave, in an undisclosed location in the mountains of Afghanistan.

- However, if you're lucky enough to be stationed at a super-FOB or COB, you may find an abundance of places to take a knee (pun intended). I've seen religious services scheduled from 0800-2000 (8:00 a.m.–8:00 p.m.) on weekends.

- The following are some examples of services offered downrange:

Paul and Kristina outside the church on FOB enjoying a nice Sunday morning.

- Catholic: including the Rosary, Reconciliation, Mass (sometimes the Canadian version)

- Protestant: including Contemporary, Church of Christ, Anglican-Episcopal, Canadian, and Gospel

- Spanish service

- LDS (Mormon) service

- Muslim prayers

• I've also seen bible study offered several times a week, sometimes tailored to particular denominations (e.g., Seventh Day Adventist) or to particular allied nations (e.g., Protestant Canadian).

• If you've never attended a religious service before or are otherwise unsure what service might be right for you, consult a chaplain for advice. They're available 24/7, and I have yet to meet an unapproachable chaplain.

Chapter 8

Relationships: Keeping It Real

*Why you'll be able to completely "let yourself go," yet still receive no
fewer than five marriage proposals . . .*

♀

One summer day, I saw what appeared to be a homeless woman.
She had dirt under her fingernails. Her hair was—for lack of a better
term—nappy, and looked as if it hadn't been washed in weeks. She
had a unibrow that extended from one side of her face to the other,
like the Brooklyn Bridge in New York City. Her skin was brown
from a layer of dirt. The hair on her upper lip would have made Fu
Manchu jealous. When she raised one arm in the air, then the other,
she exposed what I mistook for Chia Pets. She sniffed under her arms,
then raised her shirt to her nose and smelled that as well. Judging by
the look on her face, she failed the sniff test. I stood there in total awe,
thinking, "This is the most disgusting woman I've ever laid eyes on."

It wasn't until one of my fellow soldiers tapped me on the shoulder
and said "It's time to go" that I quit looking at myself in the mirror. I
thought, wow, I've really let myself go.

Later that night, I received one marriage proposal and four catcalls
on the way back to my tent. Dang, it's rough being this fine! To help
my brothers-in-arms (because some of you really need it), I offer the
following advice. If nothing else, it should keep you from having a
formal complaint filed against you—or getting shot.

Looking horrible? Don't worry!! You'll still be proposed to. *Sketch by Mike Smith*

Advice for Males Downrange: Relating to Females

* If you holler, whistle, or otherwise embarrass yourself, yet she appears to pay you no attention, it's intentional. Picking up a rock and throwing it in her direction is no way to get the kind of attention you want. One night a rock thrown in my direction, bounced once, and hit me in the leg. I was about to return fire with lethal force when the unfortunate thrower came running over to apologize.

* Don't use the following pickup lines:

  - "Are your feet tired? Because you have been running through my mind all night!"
  - "God must be weeping because heaven is missing an angel."
  - "Just call me milk: I'll do your body good!"
  - "Your name must be VISA, because it's everywhere I want to be."
  - "This could be a good night for you."
  - "Can I take you to dinner and a movie? I'm buying."

* If she obsessively touches her face with her left hand (including her ring finger), while you are talking to her, that's a hint. She's trying to gently remind you that she's married without being rude.

* If she has a knife on the table or anywhere in plain sight near her, she's a tiger waiting to pounce, so stay away. Don't question whether it's a scare tactic, because it is, and you should pay attention to it. Don't go up to her and say, "If that's meant to be a scare tactic, it's not working." You'll probably regret it!

* If you don't know her, don't invade her personal space to do any of the following: smell, touch, lick, or kiss any part of her body.

* If you say something awkward or lame, don't storm away hollering "Stupid, stupid," then come back. She'll think you either have special needs or are just weird. Either way, it won't end well for you.

* If you do find yourself a victim of sexual harassment or sexual assault, that's no laughing matter. Regardless of your gender or situation there are resources for available to you, even downrange. At a minimum there has to be at least one Sexual Harassment/Assault Response Prevention (SHARP) representative at every base downrange. Keep in mind you may also report incidents to the Chaplain, behavioral health, physician assistant, or chain of command.

♂

I'm not saying I'm actually Mr. Perfect, or even just a handsome, debonair gentleman. However, every waking moment I try to consider myself in that mindset. Seeing that this deployment of 2011 is my first deployment as a civilian, maybe it's just a money thing—it's no secret that a deployed Army civilian makes a tad bit of change.

I wish I had pictures of some of the Army females looking at me as I walk around the base or in the gym. You would have to see their eyes—the eyes of someone who is slowly undressing you, while dreaming of an alternate reality in which the two of you co-exist in blissful harmony. Then there are the subtle comments about how strenuous a seemingly easy exercise in the gym is. And the playful, kindergarten-type punches on the shoulder—just to get in a bit of physical contact.

My point is that, for those who want to start some kind of relationship, increased assertiveness is called for. Because if you're desperate, in desperate times and desperate circumstances—who can blame ya?

Why you may have more stalkers than Facebook friends . . .

♀

For most of us females downrange, it's not cool to have a fan club full of stalkers. I can't speak for all females, though. I'm no Halle Berry, but I do okay. However, it's true that some of my sisters-in-arms look like they got beat in the face with the ugly stick, and their bodies are a scientific mystery. These females may be extremely flattered, but for the rest of us. . . . Come on guys, please stop thinking you'll eventually wear us down. I had one guy on my first deployment who used to walk in circles around my MWD kennels hoping to spot me outside. I ended up throwing rocks at him, yelling, "Stay away from me, you little freak!"

Safety Tips for Female Soldiers Downrange

* Don't be overconfident! Yes, the military has taught you from the beginning to walk with authority: shoulders back, head up, and an unwavering confidence that emanates from your strength within. It's natural for you to think you're some sort of genetic mutation, a long-lost member of the X-Men possessing genes from both G.I. Joe and Wonder Woman. However, girlfriend, remember that your fellow soldiers have had the same Combatives Level 1 class you had—and are probably stronger than you. Don't unnecessarily place yourself at risk because you feel invincible.

* Remember that acquaintance rape is the most common form of rape. You never really know anybody, and that includes the battle buddies to your right and left. Try to avoid remaining alone with any male for a prolonged time. If this is not possible, keep your guard up at all times. Be prepared: always look around and identify "instruments" that you can use if you're attacked, and always know where exits are. Be situationally aware of where groups of people may be, so you can run or call for their help. This doesn't mean you should be scared of your battle buddies or alienate yourself from them out of fear. Keep in mind that many of your fellow sisters-in-arms have been victims of a sexual crime at the hands of their battle buddies, fellow soldiers, or superiors.

* Always travel with a battle buddy when possible. This may not be optional; commanders normally put in place a policy mandating that females have battle buddies during hours of limited visibility. If your battle buddy happens to be another female, don't speak when you pass by the entrance to local national army compounds during hours of darkness. If they know two females are traveling alone, they are more likely to say or do something inappropriate. I know all this is a pain in the rear, ladies, but it's for our safety.

* Don't enter local-national army territory without an escort. Yes, in many locations downrange, the black-market movies and souvenirs you may be after are sold at the local-national store within their compound. If possible, when you go, take at least one male battle buddy with you.

* Hey, Barbie, you know we're in a war zone, right? Sisters, I know some of you do this from force of habit, but try not to transform yourself into Beyoncé every morning. In a place where both "relations

with the opposite sex" and pornography are off limits, the last thing you should be doing is attempting to make yourself more attractive.

* Make sure you always have a flashlight with you, and carry a pocketknife as a secondary protection measure.

* Don't discuss your work schedule with males you don't know or the members of the local national army. Don't discuss other females' work schedules, either. You can never be too careful!

* There are cipher locks on doors to the tents, showers, and latrines for a reason. Use them, and ensure you close doors behind you.

* If you think you've ended up alone in the shower or latrine tents, use your flashlight to do a walkthrough of the tent to make sure you actually are alone before you get undressed. Power outages are common occurrences in some places, so I recommend purchasing a shower bag and placing your flashlight in it. You can hang your shower bag on the towel rack right next to you, or at least within close proximity.

Oh, I just love cheesy pickup lines. I've tried just about all of them, and the only reason I felt it would be a good idea to list some of them below is that none of them worked.

* "I've got Skittles in my mouth, wanna taste the rainbow?"

* "I'll cook you dinner if you cook me breakfast."

* "If women were trophies, you'd be first place."

* "Do you believe in love at first sight? Or do I need to walk by again?"

Why a female would be required to carry both a rape whistle and a loaded gun . . .

♀

No matter how far we've come, ladies, male soldiers in the army still have an innate, unwavering inclination to protect us. And I know that my supervisors have only the best of intentions. So, imagine my surprise on day one in my unit when my supervisor gave me a rape whistle and told me it was mandatory for all females to carry one. I took one look at that rape whistle and had two thoughts. Number 1: "Wow, it has a compass and a flashlight, cool!" Number 2: I looked at the rape whistle, then looked at my rifle, and wondered, "Why can't I just shoot him?"

Why you might be able to get away with taking a girl to dinner and a movie for free . . .

♀

If I hear "Can I take you to dinner?" or "I'm buying." one more time, I'm going to shove a chicken leg where the sun don't shine. Just so we all understand, fellas: even though this is the 21st century, and even though your boss is most likely a woman—you're still paying for a night on the town.

Hey, I know it's rough out there: the economy is bad and some people are one step away from becoming hitmen for hire just to earn a paycheck. Prices for everyday items such as gas and food continue to rise. So I understand why you (both soldiers and civilian contractors) relish any opportunity to take a woman "out" for free. And here downrange, where we service members are provided with three meals a day and the MWR or USO shows movies all day, you're loving it.

So ladies, we should do what we can to help out in these difficult economic times. We should give the guys a break. So the next time one of them offers to take you "out" downrange, return the good will and agree to go dutch!

Why some consider the combination of short shorts and hairy legs attractive (thanks, Marines!) . . .

♀

OK, I know that's not fair—the Air Force guys have some pretty short shorts, too!

♂

In desperation, the single soldier downrange will sometimes post an ad on Chemistry.com or one of the many other internet dating sites. This is done mainly in the hope that when he or she goes on leave or back to the States permanently, the newly found pen pal will be there, waiting to start a new love connection. While I find this nearly as bad an option as the private who gets married right before deployment (which usually involves buying many gifts for the new-found soulmate), the second option is probably marginally better—at least your new internet partner doesn't have access to your money yet.

Downrange, battle buddies spend many hours contemplating the best girl for each guy. Tall or short? Long hair or short? Does ethnicity matter? Would she be acceptable to take home to mom? Once you start e-mailing, how freaky is she being?

All these questions and more are often discussed in great detail when you are downrange. The person who's on the lookout often confers with the members of his whole section, those with whom he works on a daily basis.

Is true love waiting just around the corner?

♀

Don't worry, if you do happen to find that special someone online while you're downrange, there's "support" out there for you. There are several companies that target—I mean, solicit—U.S. soldiers and provide marriage by proxy. They advertise no travel necessary, completion in as little as three weeks, and provision of U.S. marriage certificates so you can get legally married even while deployed. Sorry, guys—looks like you just ran out of excuses!

Why you might, or might not, give your spouse a general power of attorney . . .

♀

As part of your pre-deployment training/clearing, you'll be given a packet containing many forms—too many to list here. One is a family pre-deployment checklist. (See our version in **Appendix 1B**.) It's designed to make your life and your family's life easier by listing all the things you should consider doing before you deploy.

One item on the list is a power of attorney for your spouse or designated representative. You can grant either a special or a general power of attorney. The Staff Judge Advocate advises against granting a general power of attorney, even to your spouse. Most soldiers don't heed that advice and grant a general power of attorney anyway.

Young, sweet, new love between two people can be a beautiful thing. Many of our young men in uniform find a special lady down at the local Walmart, and after a month come to the conclusion that they can't live the rest of their lives without her. Many of those same young, innocent soldiers end up regretting that decision.

I remember the story of one poor soldier who left his new fiancée with a general power of attorney, his debit card, and the keys to everything he owned. She decided—after just one month of being in a relationship with a deployed soldier—that the stress was too much for her. She claimed she didn't have enough money to transport herself and her things back to her hometown. So, of course, she emptied everything out of his bank account to cover the transportation costs. Noticing that his bank account was bare—he had not a single dollar to his name—he telephoned her. By the end of the conversation, some strong words had been exchanged.

What he didn't know was that she had not only cleared out his bank account but was in the process of having a garage sale. She sold everything he owned for $1.00 apiece! Poor guy. Oh, well, all's fair in love and war—right? (See **Appendix 1C** for more information on powers of attorney.)

Why you might not wear your wedding ring . . . and that it might be acceptable . . .

♂

Obviously, I'm not a female. But I would assume that if your man bought you an $8,000 engagement or wedding ring, you would NOT wear it overseas. Because if you do, it will get horribly messed up—unless you can find some way to do absolutely no work. So take my advice: before you leave, get a Walmart ring to take instead. (Unless your husband's name is Paul Smith, in which case he got you a Walmart cheapo ring in the first place. Then you just want to make sure the original doesn't get damaged—for sentimental reasons, of course.)

Guys, here's something you can do for your wives. Before you leave, go buy that cheapo ring to wear overseas, like I mentioned before. But also buy a nice little chain, and put your original wedding ring on it. Save this until the day before you depart, then give it to the love of your life so she can keep something of yours close to her heart. It will help anytime she's feeling down, having a bad day, is lonely, stressed out, or just plain missing you. (Of course, until I was writing this at this exact moment, I didn't think of applying this advice personally. Once my wife reads this, I'll probably be going to look for a nice little chain myself. I'll let you know how that goes for me another time, though.)

This is the only time you'll be allowed to take this ring off for the rest of your life, so if you've ever wanted to feel what it was like, for any reason, this is the perfect opportunity. I'm not insinuating you would do anything wrong. It's just that, for the few seconds after you take off the good ring and before you throw on your $20 temporary piece of crap, you'll notice just how much lighter your hand feels.

Additional ideas for amazing gifts or things to do before you leave are listed in **Appendix 1A**, so check it out.

In my particular case, if I had thought all this through a few months ago, I wouldn't have had the unfortunate experience of losing my own ring. Right after I got out of the army I worked at a land-based oil rig in Brighton, Colorado. So I could start training right away during the 30 days allotted for finding a more permanent place to stay, the company paid for a room at a nice Best Western. I had a successful training month and moved out into our new apartment. Then I suddenly realized that, in my excitement over getting out of the hotel, I'd left my wedding ring on the nightstand while I went to work. I hadn't wanted to mess it up while working with the pipes and doing semi-truck pre- and post-checks.

Of course, I immediately went to the hotel, where they claimed—and continued to claim for days—that they hadn't seen my ring. At that point, having held out as long as I could, I told my wife the horrid news. Surprisingly, she took it well—she just gave me that "You're so absent-minded" look.

But I was determined to find that ring. Maybe it is a cheapo Walmart ring, but it holds so much sentimental value at this point. I didn't want to let some laundry maid sell it.

I went and talked to the maids, but I found out that it's a chore if you don't know Spanish. However, after recruiting a friend of mine to overcome the language barrier, I finally found out that one of these outstanding service providers had in fact seen my ring. She suggested I inquire about its whereabouts at the front desk—where I had already asked the same question many times before. Suddenly Pablo at the front desk remembered something about a ring, and asked me to leave a callback number. I envisioned a frantic call to the local pawnshop asking his cousin to rush the ring back over because they'd been caught and it wasn't worth the $40 resale value.

So, I finally got a call and was able to pick up my ring. I thereby avoided verbal abuse on the subject for the rest of my life, involving subtle mentions during conversations with her future friends about her horrible husband who didn't care enough about his wedding ring to keep it in a safe place.

♀

Like Paul, I had a Walmart engagement/wedding ring set. I wore my rings while on base, not when outside the wire; I didn't want them to get caught on anything, or anything to happen to them that meant, God forbid, I couldn't get them back.

I did know several soldiers, both male and female, who refused to take their wedding rings off even when they went outside the wire. I remember receiving a 10-minute lecture from a guy about the sanctity of marriage, and that if I was truly committed to my husband I would wear my ring all the time. Well, after he finished, I told him off, to the effect that I wasn't aware it took a ring to make a marriage. The guy felt very small.

Sure, I'm divorced now—but I'm sure those two things weren't related. . . .

Chapter 9

Family: Keeping the Home Fires Burning

Why you'll play Call of Duty *instead of taking your children to the park—and regret it . . .*

♂

There will be a ton of things you'll need to do before you leave for Afghanistan/Iraq/Kuwait. I get it; I've been there, done that—I even helped write the book. But the things you want to do always seem to be the stupid things, the things that make no contribution to anything worthwhile—definitely not to the family. This leads to regrets after you've been gone for only two weeks.

The big one is video games. (Yes, I've played them for weeks in a row.) Remember yourself back in your living room. Think of the time your innocent little two-year-old came to you and said "pool," with his swim suit and floaties in hand. Which is most important? I know what you're thinking, but don't judge me! In any case, I may not be the most compassionate person, so I did what any dedicated gamer would do: I told him that daddy would take him after he was done—which could mean, of course, anywhere from 30 minutes to 30 hours later.

So, we didn't get to the pool that day. But thankfully my son forgot about it. He returned to his room to play with his new dinosaurs—the ones I'd picked up for him at Toys "R" Us just an hour before. My kid didn't end up crying, so this isn't that sad little story about the boy who didn't get what he wanted.

But it's little stories like this one that make you think later on. Like when you wake up after a rocket attack. Or when the warning for "Incoming!" starts playing over the speaker system. That's when you think about things, and for me it's about every time I was too busy to take Nathaniel to the pool or park, or down to the stream to throw rocks.

While you're gone, every little thing your children accomplish seems extraordinary (got two home runs; took 1st place in whatever; played in the big band concert). So, before deployment, please take part in every activity that's even close to a "big thing" for your children. Then, when junior gets on the phone with you while you're deployed and tells you about the home run he hit, you can relate in some way; you can ask, "Hey, was it as good as the one you hit in your second game?" When your little angel tells you she did all these fancy jumps while performing a dance on stage, you can say, "Great job! I bet it was even better than your performance in the *Nutcracker*."

♀

I love my family more than anything, and would do almost anything for them. However, having been deployed to downrange areas where there are MWR and USO calling centers, the willingness to actually endure "anything" can be a challenge.

In some areas there are morale centers with telephones to use for calling home. But there are a limited number of phones, so each soldier gets only 15-30 minutes to make phone calls to loved ones. I can remember waiting in line to use the telephone for nearly two hours. Then, when I finally made it to the phone booth, it took me 15 minutes to get through to an operator to connect me back to the states, so I ended up with only 15 minutes left to talk to my family.

And then, when the call finally went through, my loved one was not at home. Of course, it's not the recipients' fault—they have no idea when the soldier is going to be able to call. I know my loved ones felt just as bad about missing my call as I felt about them not being there to receive it.

Helping Kids Cope with Your Deployment

* Flat Daddy/Mommy – This is a photo of you mounted on a life-size cardboard cutout of a service member. The Flat Daddy stays at home with your family members while you deploy. They can take their Flat Daddy to special events such as graduations and birthday parties. Flat Daddies became popular at the beginning of the Iraqi war. Some units will still provide these for free to families of deployed service members. You can also apply for a free Flat Daddy at www.flatdaddies.com. If you can't get one for free, you can order one online. A Flat Daddy can cost as much as $50.00 and take up to five weeks for delivery.

* Deployment Daddy/Hug-a-Hero Doll – You upload an image of the service member, with the background removed, and it gets printed onto the front of a doll. You choose the fabric to go on the back. Depending on which website you go to, the fabric you choose, whether you choose a one- or two-sided doll, and its size, you'll pay from $20 to $70. Some of the websites will add free text to be printed below the photo; you can also order a voice recorder to be placed inside. You can apply for a free Hug-a-Hero doll at www.operationhugahero.org.

* Audio-visual – Make homemade videos or recordings prior to your service member's deployment. Pre-record videos of the service member reading books and delivering holiday messages or happy birthday wishes.

* School – Let your child's teacher(s) know about the deployment so they can assist in the transition process; it also might help explain any changed behaviors your child might exhibit. In English class they could write letters to send to you; in art class it could be drawings.

* Information control – Limit exposure to news reports, video games, and movies that depict war violence.

* Positive associations – Do special things and link them to the service member's deployment, to help create something positive out of the experience. For instance, you can mark the day of the week the service member departed by going to the park, ordering pizza, or holding game night.

* Establish a countdown mechanism. Some people paste stickers on calendars to mark off each day. Others make paper-link chains or customize calendars with family photos.

* Daddy/Mommy Clues – This basically follows the same rules as *Blue's Clues*. Scatter around some clues so your kids can follow them. Have something special waiting at the end that relates to the service member, such as a special message or one of your prerecorded video clips. When I played home-made *Blue's Clues* with my son, I used our family dog, Boomer; a small bowl; some index cards; and blue food coloring. I dipped his little Boston terrier paw into the food coloring and pressed it against the index cards. Boomer wasn't thrilled about it, but my son loved it.

* Order photo puzzles to assemble together that depict either the service member or some of your family's fondest memories. You can also use these as rewards at the end of the Daddy/Mommy Clues challenge or game night.

* Get the kids involved in sending care packages to the deployed service member. Have them help come up with lists of things to send. Include drawings, school work, and whatever else they want to send.

* Ensure you have plenty of photos of the service member hanging up around the house.

* Keep a box or scrapbook to hold the things the service member sends home. Keep it on the coffee table or somewhere else the kids can see it anytime they want.

* Keep things as close to normal as possible. Try to maintain the usual routine so the children can see that life does go on even with the service member gone. Continue family traditions.

* Military One Source has several resources for military families. One is their Military Youth on the Move, http://apps.militaryonesource.mil/MOS/f?p=MYOM:HOME2:0. Their subcategories cover everything from moving out, healthy living, getting help, and staying safe geared for kids as young as 6 to teenagers. Your children can even chat with other military children online. Within their Get Help category they address issues that surround deployments for military children.

However, it did mean I had wasted 2 ½ hours of my day trying to call—for nothing. When you're deployed, are going out on missions, and are constantly stressed, this is just one more thing to throw on the pile. So there were times I could have called my family, but didn't feel like waiting in line for two hours just to be disappointed in the end. I know that may sound harsh, but it's the truth for many soldiers out there.

Why you'll be excited when your webpage takes only 10 minutes to load, or the phones don't drop your calls, or the delay time is no more than five seconds . . .

♂

Let's consider an example: Say you're ordering flowers for your loved one back home. But you're constantly being asked "What did you say?" because they don't get the concept that there's a delay over the phone line, so they constantly talk while you're trying to answer. Once it took almost half an hour for me to place an order; we didn't make much progress until the lady finally realized where I was.

Don't bother trying to upload even a short video clip, unless you're prepared to spend the next half hour of your life waiting—which, by the way, is about your time limit at the computer station, so you may not even have time left to watch it. My advice: ask your loved ones to just send you the picture of your son with cake all over his mouth; it'll probably be less painful than trying to pull it up on Facebook.

I hope that one of these days certain companies and banks start to understand that some of their devoted customers are going away for a year. Props to some of them, such as CenturyLink, that have an online chat function, which in my experience is open 24/7 and allows me to get everything I need taken care of at a decent hour for me.

In contrast: Hey, banks—what's the deal? Unless a solder has banking online, he's going to have to call you. Most days, staying up until two or three in the morning is not an option just so the call will arrive at a decent time for you in the States. Apparently, calling you on the weekends is also not an option you'd like to extend, because, unlike us, your weekend is spent at home cuddled up with your family. If you start losing business to the more military-friendly banks, don't say I didn't warn you.

Here's another happy little subject (especially for those wives who can't seem to live without a call from or to their loved ones): blackouts. That means no phones and no internet. I'm not sure how much I can say about this subject. Suffice it to say, when someone gets hurt, regardless of the circumstances, the family needs to be notified. (It's important for the family to be informed directly instead of hearing about it from Private Joe Snuffy, who'll probably get the facts wrong.) To make that happen, all other phone and computer access to the outside world gets cut off for a period that can range from hours to days.

Why you may regret not teaching your spouse how to . . .

In my case, this section should probably be labeled "what she should have taught me." I'm lucky in that I don't have to worry the lawn won't get mowed because she can't figure out how to pull on the cord thingamabob.

But most wives don't know where the gas goes, for instance. And if they can figure that out, "What is the choke?" will likely be the next question.

For my last deployment, I was a "late deployer" by a month or so, and that got me thinking. As I drove around the base, there were a lot of unmowed lawns. Driving to the post office one day, I made a wrong turn and ended up in a particular neighborhood on Ft. Carson. (I'll leave the road and person un-named.) There I stumbled across a most awkward scene.

Picture, for a moment, a tall, slender, blonde, mid-twenties housewife standing on her front lawn. She's wearing what looks to be a Sunday dress, with three-inch heels. She's also wearing a most puzzled look—the kind with one eyebrow up and the other down. She's half-staring down at a bright red push lawn mower. I stop and observe for a moment. She reaches down, grasps the string, and pulls with all her force—seven or eight times. By this point, sweat is dripping down her whole body, and she looks to be close to dehydration.

I get out of my vehicle and ask what the problem is. She explains that she's attempting to mow the lawn for the first time, so far it's been a total failure, and she would be happy at this point to just get the thing started.

I ask the obvious question: does it have fuel? She answers politely, "Oh, I forgot to check." Luckily for her, it does have some, so I don't have to embarrass her in that department.

The next few steps, however, reveal her true level of expertise. I ask her where the primer bulb is. After admitting she doesn't know, she pulls out a piece of paper to start taking notes. Next I depress the choke starter, at which point she comments, "Oh, I was wondering what that was for." I remain polite, making no comment.

Finally I pull the cord and, to her surprise, it works. After a few more lessons on the startup procedure, I walk back to my car.

At this point, I feel like I've just accomplished the greatest feat known to man: I taught something to a true blonde! And I mean, not just a blonde, but a true, the-kind-jokes-are-made-about blonde.

A similar story: when I was home on leave during my first deployment, a friend of mine called from Iraq and asked me to go over to his house and help his wife with a problem. Being the awesome battle buddy I am, of course I went running to his wife's aid. Except I wasn't actually running, because it had snowed the previous day, leaving a nice, thin, slippery layer of ice on the ground.

I rolled up to the house. The first thing I noticed was that her car wasn't all the way in the driveway—it was halfway in the road. I walked to the house, slipping and sliding the entire way up the walkway to the door. When she came to the door, she was very happy to see me.

She immediately pointed to her car. I mustered a, "Yeah, I noticed." She explained she'd been unable to pull it in because of the ice, and needed help to get it out of the road. I asked whether she'd put down any rock salt the previous night. Of course, the answer was, "No, what's that?"

Luckily I had my truck with me, so I gave the car a gentle push into the driveway. I then spent a few minutes explaining the concept of salt, or its equivalent (those environmentally friendly ice-melting pellet bags). Next I brought over a snow shovel for her to use the next day, seeing that she barely understood the oh-so-complicated salting process. I stuck around long enough that she was able to sucker me into shoveling the snow off the driveway for her.

For some reason, I never returned her calls again. A fun fact: this woman just happened to be another one of those tall, slender, long-haired blondes. The only difference between this one and the one in the previous story is that this one decided to procreate. I feel so sorry for those children; I've often thought about kidnapping them to ensure they don't end up with their mother's "enormous" IQ.

Now, I'm not trying to insult anyone's intelligence. But gents, you're going to end up paying for even the small things that go wrong. When your spouse can't figure it out, she's going to call the contractor. And don't expect it to get done for the cheapest rates around, either.

Why you may complain every day about missing home, but can't manage to pack up when the time comes . . .

♀

All right! Day after day, week after week, month after endless month, you've hoped, you've prayed, you've wished upon every star in the Middle Eastern sky for time to magically fly by so you could get the heck out of there. Now that time has finally arrived! You're one week out from the TOA (transfer of authority) ceremony, and your replacement is here, so you can finally RIP (relieve/relief in place).

But it's the darnedest thing: you haven't managed to pack a thing. You still have at least one box of must-have essentials (*Scooby Doo* comforter, sheets, last-minute souvenirs, your kids' drawings, things that you've "acquired" downrange, etc.) that you need to mail out. You've been avoiding doing that because every time you've walked by the post office there's been a line snaking around the building, made up of other procrastinating soldiers like yourself. You're terrified that at any moment your First Sergeant will do a tent inspection and find out that you're a long way from living out of your duffle.

What the heck is wrong with you? You've spent at least 10 minutes of every day wishing you had a flux capacitor to make time travel possible, so you could install it in your MRAP and end the deployment. You've managed to complain about everybody and everything until there is nothing left to complain about. You've had the "What's the first thing you're going to do when you get home?" conversation at least 23 times, and have narrowed it down to one of three: sex, sleep, or the consumption of an alcoholic beverage.

Don't panic: you're not alone—many soldiers fall into this trap. And it's not your fault that somewhere, in a twisted part of your mind, you've somehow managed to get comfortable in this place. So, while at dinner chow in the DFAC, you sit back, zone out, and contemplate the reasons this could be happening:

1. You're lazy, too tired, or both. You want to leave, but you don't want to make the effort to do it. You're also worn out from long hours and stress, and possibly shell shocked from the repeated rounds of IDF fired at your base or mission-related insurgent attacks. Just the thought of having to lug your brigade-mandated packing list from FOB to FOB, from transient tent to transient tent, leaves you exhausted.

2. You're attempting to avoid something back home—or at least delay having to face it. Unfortunately, even though you may feel invincible at times, you're not immune to life's unfortunate events. Perhaps your relationship has ended, or it may be in the process of ending. You may have lost a loved one, and you know that when you return home but don't and can't see that person, it will be devastating for you. There can be any number of issues you've managed to put off dealing with for several months because you've been downrange, but now, as you're heading home, the realization of them has hit you like a ton of bricks.

3. You've changed. The change could be for better or worse. In either case, you're afraid of what that might mean. Maybe you wonder whether you'll still feel the same way about your significant other. Maybe you think you might have post-traumatic stress disorder (PTSD), but are afraid to admit it. Maybe you've grown spiritually and have committed to

adopting a different lifestyle when you get back. You may not feel comfortable talking about any of this with your battle buddies because you don't want them to think you're weak, but you can definitely sense that something is different.

4. Right now, downrange feels more like home than back home does. Downrange, everybody is somebody's brother or sister. You've forged relationships built out of the blood of combat, relationships that no one other than your battle buddies could understand. You don't want to lose those relationships, you don't want all of that to change. You fear that once you all get back to the rear, you'll reunite with your loved ones and go your separate ways.

The good news is, these feelings and thoughts are normal—you're not alone! As you go through the process of integrating into your "normal" life, you'll work through it. Both before redeployment and during reverse Soldier Readiness Center/Checklist (SRC), you'll attend classes on the stages of return/reunion.

Why you may get a chance to realize you can still get embarrassed . . .

♂

So, you're on your way home after the first six months of your year-long tour. When you step on board your first civilian flight home, you finally see faces that are completely new to you, of people who have nothing to do with the military. As you walk down the aisle to your seat, you see a hand come out. The voice that goes along with that hand praises you for what you're doing. This appreciation seems to start a chain reaction. Your seat is at back of the plane, so just about every person gets a chance to shake your hand and thank you. Finally you put your bags in the overhead compartment and sit down. You take a long, deep, satisfying breath, knowing you'll be home soon.

Then an elderly lady gets up and starts to walk all the way to the back of the plane. She has a cane in one hand, and looks as if she's having some trouble walking. As she approaches, you're curious about the paper she's holding in her other hand. She tells you that the seat you're sitting in doesn't befit your service and the sacrifice you've made for your country—and she hands you her business-class ticket. After five minutes of telling her you'd feel bad about taking it, her sincerity convinces you. You thank her and make the long walk back up to business class. As you pass by, you hear a boy of maybe six or seven ask his mother in a soft voice, "Mommy, is he the one on the news helping overseas?" You don't stick around long enough to find out her answer, mainly because you don't feel deserving of all this praise.

The rules say you're not supposed to have any alcoholic beverages on the flight back, but after the plane takes off a rather hearty fellow who kind of reminds you of your grandpa offers you a beer. You dutifully explain that it's not allowed, but he says, "Hogwash! How are you going to get what you want with that kind of attitude? Sometimes you have to bend the rules." Just to appease the man, you politely drink the nine-dollar beer he paid for and listen to stories from his Vietnam War days.

Suddenly the plane jerks, and you find that at some point you must have been so exhausted you fell asleep. The tray table in front of you is down, with your dinner sitting on it. And there's a letter, too. It reads:

Dear Super Hero,
    My mommy says you're the one on the news all the time. Thank you for beating up the bad guys. You do good work.
                                                                    Johnny

You assume Johnny was the boy you passed earlier, but once you land you find out for sure. The captain asks you to stay on the plane because there are still a few passengers who want the chance to shake your hand, and you agree. The little boy is one of the last to leave the plane. When he comes up, he says, "I'll be praying for you"—accompanied by the biggest chocolate-covered smile you can imagine.

Your wife—like so many of your friends' wives, at this point—is pregnant. When you meet at the airport, you're shocked to see how much bigger your baby boy has gotten—he should be coming along any day now! This vacation time couldn't have come at a better moment.

After a hundred kisses and "I missed you so much!" your bags are finally in the car. You're on your way home!

Why you'll realize you've forgotten how to do the simplest tasks . . .

♂

Here are some examples of simple but forgotten aspects of normal daily life that may require a little readjustment when you get back:

- When I got back to the states, I honestly had to take a second look at the road signs. I'd almost forgotten how to drive like a normal person. I could easily have gotten pulled over during my first week back home, because I'm sure it looked as if I'd just left the local bar so intoxicated I should have been in the drunk tank. For at least a few seconds there I'm pretty sure I was driving down the center of the road as if I was in an assault vehicle. And I probably wasn't even wearing my seatbelt!

- Who in his right mind likes making a grocery list for a family of three? But when you've only had to worry about yourself for an entire year and mostly survived on pre-made meals, this little job could turn into a half-day project. How many gallons of milk do I get? Let's see, I'm used to drinking about two gallons a week myself (I really like my milk), so, multiply that times three, right? Nope, bought way too much.

- Stop looking down at your side and thinking you forgot your weapon somewhere. Once I spent a good 20 minutes looking around my own home for the M4 that wasn't there, for obvious reasons.

- If a friend slams the freaking door one more time, I swear I will go hysterical on his ass. It's not funny, people—seriously.

One other thing: I appreciate everybody's consideration, I really do. But why on God's green earth do you have to tell someone you've been overseas before they start to help you? On the other hand, when you've forgotten how to do so much while you were away, how else are you going to get what you need taken care of in a timely manner?

Points to Remember During Reintegration

Service members and loved ones should keep the following things in mind during reintegration. Note: this list is not all-inclusive, additional resources are listed in **Appendix 3E**.

* Service members and loved ones may have changed. Deployments are a life-altering event, not only for the service member but for loved ones as well. Either one of you could have changed physically, emotionally, or mentally. Service members need to be patient with friends and family and realize that it may take time to reconnect with them. Understand that just because something has changed or is different, that doesn't make it wrong. Sometimes, as Sheryl Crow sings, "A change will do you good."

* Households and surroundings may have changed. While the service member was gone, somebody else had to step up. Maybe the loved one is now paying the bills, whereas it used to be the service member. Maybe the eldest boy now mows the lawn and takes the trash out instead of the service member. Service members need to ease back into their roles within the household and discuss any changes that have been made. Realize that roles and responsibilities in the household may never go back to the way they were. Some military families may have had to PCS (carry out a permanent change of station—a move) without the service member. So the service member returns home to a brand-new home or location. Things that were once familiar are now foreign to the service member.

* There may be some awkwardness in personal relationships, and intimacy with significant others may take time. Six months to a year without any "adult time" with your significant other can drive anyone crazy. In your mind, you've played out the scene of your first night back together time and time again. Like two wild animals you go at it— like "gorillas in the mist." However, when the time finally does come, one or both of you may feel a little awkward, like two teens on prom night. Relax; sometimes it takes a while to rekindle those old flames.

Remember: intimacy is about the closeness you feel as a couple, not just about sex.

* Service members or family members may feel that they need space. Wait a minute—you just spent a year away from each other, yet somehow you find yourselves in two different rooms watching TV?! Don't worry that this means you don't love each other or didn't miss each other. While the service member was downrange, you all got used to doing whatever you wanted in your spare time. Perhaps the loved one got a job or joined a club while the service member was away. Just because the service member has returned, that doesn't mean he or she has to now quit those things. You can still have a loving relationship without spending every minute of your life together.

* The service member may have difficulty sleeping. The first thing to remember is that he or she radically changed time zones. A military family life consultant (MFLC) informed me that for each hour of time zone difference, it takes at least a day to get back to normal. So you can expect your sleep schedule to be off for eight to eleven days after your return. This is the simplest explanation for why the service member is waking up often or having trouble sleeping. Also keep in mind that the service member is adjusting to different sounds and smells. Whereas he used to fall asleep to the smell of the burn pit and the sound of an unmanned aerial vehicle (UAV) taking flight, now *The Late Show* is on and you smell like flowers—that could take some getting used to. However, if he or she has repeated nightmares about incidents that happened downrange, seek professional help.

* Loved ones may be resentful about deployments even when they've ended, and service members may feel guilty for having been gone. Perhaps a child was sick, or the loved one had a difficult time trying to do everything while the service member was away. But it doesn't do anybody any good to feel guilty about circumstances that no one had any control over. You, the military family, chose this life, and there are some things that just can't be helped.

* The service member may go through a range of emotions. He or she may feel constantly tired or unmotivated. There has been a loss of the adrenaline that was needed downrange. Service members may feel angry or frustrated due to the stress of change. Arguments may occur. Just remember, this emotional roller coaster that service members and loved ones can go through is normal. While in an argument with your significant other or otherwise angry, avoid disciplining, or even engaging, a child. The U.S. military has a zero-tolerance policy

regarding spousal or child abuse; besides, you're better than that. Approach each situation calmly, and be receptive to what the other person has to say.

* Service members may feel jealousy at how close the other parent has become to children, and may feel hurt by how young children do—or don't— receive them. Reassure the service member that he or she is in fact loved by all. Arrange for "alone time" with each family member to reconnect.

* The service member should be respectful of others when discussing deployment experiences. Your Aunt Maddy may not think it's cool that you kicked a door in and placed two in the chest of an insurgent at an IED-making factory. Service members, remember the audience you're addressing when you tell your war stories. On the opposite end of the spectrum, service members may not want to talk about their deployment at all, and family members shouldn't try to force them to do so. Perhaps they watched a battle buddy die or had to commit a violent act they'd rather not remember. You can encourage service members to talk about the war, and you can provide support and let them know you're there for them—then let whatever happens, happen.

* Service members, be sure to take care of yourself physically. In particular, avoid excessive drinking, and never turn to drugs as a way of coping with your situation. Don't be afraid to talk about what you're going through and what you're feeling, including to other military families. Believe that you're loved by many—family, friends, your fellow service members, and the citizens of a grateful nation. Realize that there is help out there, and don't be afraid to seek it if needed. Realize that your loved ones may be struggling as well, and be alert to changes in their behavior. The same services available for service members are also available for family members. Remember, no matter how bad you may be hurting, suicide is never the answer. If you suspect that a service member or loved one may be considering suicide, remember the Army's acronym for suicide intervention, ACE:

- **A**sk your buddy
  - Have the courage to ask the question, but stay calm
  - Ask the question directly, e.g., "Are you thinking of killing yourself?"
- **C**are for your buddy
  - Remove any means that could be used for self-injury

- Calmly control the situation; do not use force
- Actively listen to produce relief
- **E**scort your buddy
  - Never leave your buddy alone
  - Escort your buddy to the chain of command, a chaplain, a behavioral health professional, or a primary care provider

Preparation

1A: Things to Explain to Your Wife/Husband

After consulting many deployed husbands and other service members, I came up with the following list of actual things that have fallen between the cracks after a soldier is deployed and the spouse is left behind. They may all seem easy to learn, but one person took them for granted because his or her significant other had always been there to perform them. Guys, make sure your wife knows about these things, so someone like me can't come along later and joke about it in a book!

- Mowing the lawn. (See **Chapter 9**)

- Checking the smoke detectors.

- Operating the water pump (in case the basement floods).

- Contacting utilities maintenance and repairmen.

- Paying the bills. (They won't pay themselves.)

- Operating the alarm system.

- Changing all the filters in the house.

- Operating the fireplace. (This may also involve teaching your spouse how to use the chainsaw.)

- Contacting Rear Detachment (Rear D) and the Red Cross. (Trust me, they forget how.)

- Installing propane tank onto gas grill (without burning your eyebrows off).

- Deep-frying a frozen turkey. (On second thought, please don't attempt this at all!)

- Limiting the number of things plugged into the socket behind the Christmas tree (so it doesn't reach a million).

- Taking dogs (at least big ones) OUTSIDE for walks. (Yes, I realize a dog is man's best friend, but he's not home.)

- Shoveling snow. (This too can be a surprisingly complicated task, so the gym may be a good idea for you ladies who insist on using only your back.)

- Checking the air pressure in the car's tires. (Ridin' on 20" rims? You'll need to know how.)

- Changing the oil in the car(s) (or at least knowing when it needs to get done).

- Scraping your windshield in cold weather. (Oh, by the way: pouring hot water on it will probably crack it.)

- Handling guns safely. (Taking your spouse to a shooting range is probably a good idea.)

- Checking/relighting the pilot light on the stove and/or water heater.

- Operating the circuit breaker or fuse box.

- Preparing for the zombie apocalypse or a natural disaster.

- Accessing medical care.

♀

Oh no you don't! Don't worry, ladies, I picked up on Paul's smart remarks, and I've addressed some of his "concerns" and made a little list of my own.

- Washing the dishes. (This can be surprisingly complicated, especially if you own a dishwasher.)

- Putting out a grease fire (so when he decides to deep-fry dinner in a skillet, he won't burn the house down).

- Bailing the water out of the basement when it floods. (Buy him plenty of buckets.)

- Contacting utilities maintenance and repairmen. (If Tim "the Tool Man" Taylor from the TV show *Home Improvement* reminds you of your husband, I feel sorry for you. You know the type: he's seen one too many episodes of *This Old House* and has decided he's a handyman. How many items does he have on his project list? When he finally gets around to "fixing" something around the house, do you really wish he hadn't? Does the faucet that used to drip now run? When he last "fixed" the doorbell, did he electrocute himself? Does the crown molding he installed now have a huge gap between it and the ceiling, serving as a constant reminder of how "handy" he is? Make sure both of you have the list of phone numbers, so when he "misplaces" the list you'll be able to square him away.)

- Paying the bills. (Make sure he understands the priorities: that food, shelter, and the children's needs come before PlayStation games and new gadgets.)

- Balancing the checkbook. (Make sure he knows that eventually the ATM will stop spitting out money if there's no more in the account.)

- Operating the security system. (To us ladies, a security alarm means a computerized system designed to detect unauthorized entry into a property. Unfortunately for males, it means either a baseball bat or a firearm. Or worse, they refer to their two fists as "dynamite and titanium." Plus, every time you bring up the subject of an alarm/security system, they tell you there's no need, flex their muscles, and ask whether you've purchased tickets to the gun show. So make sure he remembers to practice firearm safety, especially if there are children in the home. And invite the security system folks over to pitch the importance of having an actual system.)

- Changing the toilet paper roll! (This too must be a complicated task, because so many men seem to be incapable of completing it; but it's necessary on so many levels.)

- Operating the fireplace. (When men get frustrated because they can't get a fire started, copious quantities of lighter fluid are NOT the answer!)

- Phoning important contacts. (Tape important numbers somewhere near each telephone in the house. Trust me, if there's just one list, he'll forget where he put it. I suggest affixing the list to the wall, because what will happen if he needs a phone number but has placed a magazine or the mail on top of the nice, organized list you compiled for him? You won't be there to pick up those items to show him where the list is after he claims he can't find it.)

- Installing the propane tank onto the gas grill. (Either sit down and read him the installation instructions, or make sure one of his buddies who has owned and safely operated a propane grill helps him out—so his eyebrows don't get burnt off!)

- How to cook something using a method other than deep-frying. (That trip last summer to the state fair didn't help your cause, when he ate deep-fried Twinkies and candy bars and drank (ate) a deep-fried margarita. Leave your man some simple, easy-to-follow recipes for healthy family dishes.

Point him to the internet where there are plenty of step-by-step instructional videos for healthy recipes. When in doubt, refer him to YouTube.)

- Limiting the number of things plugged into the socket behind the Christmas tree. (Images come to mind of the father on *A Christmas Story* when he tries to plug in his "award"—a laced woman's leg lamp—behind the Christmas tree. Chevy Chase in *National Lampoon's Christmas Vacation* stringing up his annual Christmas lights extravaganza is also a popular image. Please ensure your man watches both of these movies prior to the most joyful of holiday seasons—so you won't need a Christmas miracle for your family and house to survive!)

- Walking the kids. (Big kids need to go for walks outside and play at the park. So, when he takes the dog for a walk, make sure he knows to bring the kids along, too.)

- Performing household chores. (This can be a complicated process. Guys, you might want to go to the gym and look into some yoga classes. As any stay-at-home mom can tell you, doing this job is a balancing act that takes a lot of flexibility. To maintain a home **and** take care of the children requires discipline, a strong work ethic, creativity, mental and physical strength, and the ability to think on your feet and multitask. Good luck, guys!)

- Checking the air pressure in the car's tires. (Ridin' on 20" rims? You'll need to know how. If you and your man are under the age of 35, there's a good chance you know as much about vehicle maintenance as he does. The only real difference is that it's still expected and acceptable for women not to know anything about cars. Yes, as the feminist movement progressed to the point where we almost had our first female president, we got more independent. We started looking under the hood and wondering what's that noise, where's that smell coming from, and what does this thingy do? At the same time, guys noticed us looking under the hood and many of them stopped wondering. One time while traveling I struck an object that blew out one of my tires. While I was changing my tire, two male Jehovah's Witnesses who had seen my near-fatal accident pulled over and insisted on changing my tire for me. They were sweet guys, and I really appreciated it—but I had to coach the young men through the whole process. So make sure you print out MapQuest directions to the Goodyear store, just in case. This is also cost-effective, ladies! Gas prices are through the roof, and it could cost a fortune in gas if you don't ensure he knows the way—because he'll surely drive around for hours rather than stop and ask directions.)

- Changing diapers. (Babies need this! Make sure he knows how to take care of your children. You'll worry anyway, but you'll worry less if you're confident he has the basics down. Arrange for your mom or his mom or some similarly knowledgeable person to be available to contact if he runs into a question or emergency.)

- Acknowledging special occasions. (Not sending you at least a card for your birthday, anniversary, or other special date while you're overseas will put him in the doghouse, so do your man a favor and leave him a list of special events. That way he won't have to guess, and he'll have time to plan things. The mail travels slowly, and if he thinks your anniversary is in August he'll wait until July to send you something, but if in reality your anniversary is in July whatever he sends will be late.)

- Handling guns safely. (Taking your spouse to a shooting range is probably a good idea.)

- Checking/relighting the pilot light on the stove and/or water heater. (First, point out the stove and list its many benefits. Try to sell him on the idea that eating microwavable meals every day will likely lead to irritable bowel syndrome—and you won't be there to take care of him when he's sick.)

- Operating the washer and dryer. (See **Chapter 5** on why it's acceptable for other people (besides your mother) to do your laundry. Unfortunately ladies, Paul's story is all too common. Your son could end up leaving the house in pink t-shirts because your husband mixed the colors and whites again.)

- Preparing/drilling for a natural disaster (and stop practicing the zombie apocalypse drill with the children).

- Accessing medical care when little Billy breaks his leg. (Probably while he's attempting to re-enact everything his father told him he did as a child. Purchase safety equipment for the children for when their father decides to play circus with them and tosses them across the room. Get helmets and knee and elbow pads to use on the homemade skateboard/bike ramps they'll build while you're away, and for when they fall out of the tree their father let them climb all the way to the top. Ensure the kids know how to dial 911 so when their father shows them how he used to jump off the roof of his house as a kid, the children can call the ambulance for him.)

1B: Pre-Deployment Checklist

Although deployments are never easy, anything you can do to help your family out while you're away will be beneficial to both you and them. It's difficult for soldiers to concentrate on the task at hand if they're constantly wondering whether their families are OK. Encourage them to keep originals or copies of all listed documents where they can easily access them.

I used a checklist to put together a "deployment book" for my mother while I was gone. I made copies of all the documents and enclosed them in a binder. I also included step-by-step instructions on how to pay the bills. My mother loved it and found it very helpful.

Documents

- Current Armed Forces identification cards of dependents.

- Medical (including shot) and dental records of all family members and pets.

- Birth certificates for all family members.

- Marriage certificates.

- Power of attorney (POA). See **Appendix 1C** for POA types.

- Civilian life insurance policies.

- Emergency data card/DD 93.

- Wills for both spouses and service member's burial wishes.

- Social Security cards for family members.

- Tax returns—both state and federal—for the previous two years, at a minimum. (The IRS requires a POA, obtained only from them, which allows the spouse to file taxes.)

- Copies of orders.

- Last leave and earnings statement (LES).

- Adoption papers.

- Passports and visas (if your family plans to travel to an overseas area).

- Citizenship/naturalization papers.

- Divorce papers.

- Title for the car (know where it's located).

- Car registration (for both on and off post).

- Real estate documents (leases, mortgages, deeds, promissory notes).

- Emergency contact list (including telephone numbers and addresses of close friends, your personal lawyer, and unit contact information for the Rear D).

- Telephone book, for both on and off the military installation. (Mark the numbers of emergency agencies such as Army Emergency Relief, the Red Cross, chaplains, legal assistance, military police, medical facilities, Tricare, Army Community Service, etc.)

Miscellaneous

- Tricare: Are all dependents enrolled? Do family members know where to go for medical/dental treatment?

- If anyone in your family has special medical needs, are they enrolled in the Exceptional Family Member Program?

- Is your wife pregnant? If so, when is she due? (Ensure the service member has a statement from her doctor, especially if she's expected to have a problem pregnancy.)

- Is your spouse on the deed to your home? (If the service member passes away, the surviving spouse may have to put the house through probate if and when he/she tries to sell it, even if the service member had a will.)

- Servicemembers Group Life Insurance (SGLI): Decide whether your coverage is sufficient; if not, consider purchasing additional life insurance. (SGLI is available in increments of $10,000 up to a maximum of $400,000. The U.S. Army provides a one-time, lump-sum death gratuity of $100,000 to the primary next of kin of a soldier who dies while on active duty.)

- Does your spouse have a driver's license? A car? (If not, ensure he/she has some form of transportation for errands, emergencies, etc.)

- Does the car registration/license plate need to be renewed while you're gone? If so, does your spouse know how to renew it?

- Is your auto insurance up to date?

- Do your dependents know where to go for car repairs? Does your vehicle have a warranty, and does your spouse know what's covered?

- Does your vehicle have an emergency kit (i.e., flashlight, first aid kit, blankets, water, food, tools, ice scraper, etc.)?

- Does your spouse know how to perform emergency car repairs, such as changing a tire?

- Do you have an emergency kit in your house (i.e., flashlights, candles, fire extinguisher, matches, extra batteries, bottled water, etc.)?

- Does your family have a fire evacuation plan for your home?

- Do your spouse and children know how to contact emergency services (i.e., fire department, police, 911)?

- Does your spouse have access to your financial records (i.e., checkbook, credit cards, debit cards)? See **Appendix 2B**.

- Does your spouse know how to execute your finance plan. (List companies' names, contact information, payment information, and account numbers.) See **Appendix 2C**.

- Do you have a safe deposit box? Does your spouse know the location of the key?

1C: Power of Attorney

Source of information: the Fort Leonard Wood SJA. See www.wood.army.mil/sja/LA/power_of_attorney.htm.

Definition: A POA is a written instrument that allows you (the "principal") to authorize your agent (your "attorney-in-fact") to conduct certain business on your behalf. A POA is one of the strongest legal documents you can give to another person. Every act performed by your agent within the authority of the POA is legally binding upon you. Since a POA is such a powerful document, give it only to a trustworthy person, and only when absolutely necessary.

Considerations Regarding All POAs

- A POA becomes void upon the death of the principal.

- A POA normally is void if the principal becomes physically or mentally incapacitated. However, appropriate "durability" language may be added to the POA to ensure it will remain valid during any period of incapacity.

- Any third party has the right to refuse to accept a POA.

- A POA should be given for only a limited period (such as six months during a deployment). A third party is more likely to accept a POA with a recent date than one that is outdated.

- Many financial institutions and other businesses have their own POAs that they prefer to be used to conduct business. It's a good idea to show your POA to all known third parties who may be dealing with your named attorney-in-fact to ensure your POA will be acceptable to them.

- Your appointee or agent must have the original POA; you should keep a copy for your records.

- You may revoke a POA before its expiration date by executing a revocation of the POA. Notice of the revocation must be delivered to the attorney-in-fact, as well as to all third parties who you know relied on the POA. If possible, recover from the attorney-in-fact and destroy the original and all copies of the POA. Even though the POA has been revoked, you may be responsible to any third party who did not receive notice of the revocation.

Types of POAs

• A general POA gives your agent very broad powers to act on your behalf; a special POA limits your agent's authority to act only on certain matters.

• You may hear that you need a general POA so that someone else can take care of all your affairs when you're absent. This is probably not true; in fact, it's highly unlikely you'll ever need a general POA. Never give a general POA when a special POA will accomplish the mission. There is less opportunity for abuse when only limited powers are given.

• A special POA should be as specific as possible. For example, if you are authorizing an attorney-in-fact to sell a vehicle on your behalf, specify the vehicle, license number, vehicle identification number, the make/model/year of the vehicle, and any specific terms you will require.

• Your legal assistance attorney can advise you about POAs and help you tailor a POA to suit your precise situation and needs.

General Power of Attorney: A general POA gives your agent the authority to do most things you could do yourself, such as write checks and pay bills, borrow money, and sign contracts in your name. Your agent cannot perform certain actions that require your personal attention, such as taking an oath. General POAs may not be accepted for performing certain acts, such as cashing goverment checks or conducting real estate transactions.

Special (Limited) Power of Attorney: A special, or limited, POA authorizes your agent to do only a specified act, such as sell your car, ship your household goods, or cash your paycheck. Such a POA can accomplish almost any need: access to a particular bank account; closing on a house; medical care for your children; or movement of your household goods. The special POA is more likely to be accepted by those with whom the individual you have designated will be trying to do business. Because it is drawn for a specific purpose, it is often considered to be a more reliable measure of your actual intent. Some acts may only be accomplished with a special POA. For example, authorizing someone to buy or sell real estate in your name requires a special POA that describes, in great detail, the property and the specific acts to be done by your agent. Here is a description of the normal types of special powers:

Financial

- Cash checks: To endorse, cash, and receive the proceeds of any check or other negotiable instrument.

- File claims: To institute and prosecute, or to appear and defend, any claims or litigation involving me.

- Start, stop, or change an allotment.

- Receive my leave and earning statement(s).

- Borrow money from service relief organizations (e.g., Army Emergency Relief).

Quarters

- Accept military quarters, including signing and taking possession.

- Clear/terminate quarters.

Household goods

- Ship household goods, personal baggage, or other personal property.

- Accept delivery of, and receipt for, household goods and/or unaccompanied baggage.

Real property

- Sell, buy, rent/lease, or manage, mortgage.

Motor vehicle

- Use and operate, sell, buy, ship, or accept delivery.

Child(ren)

- Temporary custody, loco parentis/education enrollment.

- To do all acts necessary or desirable for maintaining the health, education, and welfare of my child, including the registration and enrollment of my child in educational programs and schools.

- To maintain the customary living standard of my child, including, but not limited to, provisions of living quarters, food, clothing, medical, surgical and dental care, entertainment and other customary matters.

- Specifically, to approve and authorize any and all medical treatment deemed necessary by a duly licensed physician and to execute any consent, release, or waiver of liability required by medical or dental authorities incident to the provision of medical, surgical, or dental care to my child, by qualified medical personnel.

- To act in loco parentis to [name/date of birth of child(ren)].

Medical care

- To do all that is necessary or desirable for maintaining the health of my child(ren).

- Specifically, to approve and authorize any and all medical treatment deemed necessary by a duly licensed physician and to execute any consent, release, or waiver of liability required by medical or dental authorities incident to the provision of medical, surgical, or dental care to my child(ren) by qualified medical personnel.

Special Power of Attorney to Act "In Loco Parentis": This is a common type of special POA. The phrase *in loco parentis* means "in the place of the parent." Such a POA grants parental authority to another (such as a babysitter) to perform a range of functions that can include picking up a child from school, buying food and clothing, and consenting to medical treatment of the child in the event of illness or injury. If you have children, you will almost surely want a special POA to provide for their non-emergency medical care when you and your spouse are away. Service medical regulations clearly provide that your children may be treated if a true emergency exists and you or your spouse cannot be reached. In a non-emergency situation, however, consent is required before treatment. The special medical POA is, in effect, your transfer of your authority to consent to that treatment to another individual whom you have chosen to act for you. You cannot designate a medical facility; you must designate a specific person, or two, alternatively—for example, a husband and wife, either of whom you would trust with decisions concerning medical care for your children. The individual you designate must be an adult.

Without this type of special POA, a day care center, school, store, hospital, or clinic, fearing legal repercussions, may refuse to follow the directives of the babysitter or other agent, and require the specific authorization of the actual parent. This grant of authority will assist the agent in the daily business of looking after the child, and can avoid unnecessary delays in emergencies. Furthermore, the special

POA provides legal protection for the facility, and also for the agent who might otherwise fear taking action on behalf of the child.

Your legal assistance attorney can prepare the "in loco parentis" special POA.

1D: Things To Do Before Departure

- Provide your spouse/significant other with whatever type of POA you mutually decide upon. (See **Appendix 1C**)

- Get your bank contact information. (Just in case your spouse goes crazy with that POA.)

- Play with your dog. (You can't be sure a downrange dog is rabies-free.)

- Search the internet about camel spiders. (Are they really as big as Sgt. Snuffy said? Will they really suck your blood?)

- Learn why the Total Gym guy is so cool.

- Download a copy of the *Top Gun* song "Danger Zone" to your iPod. (It just feels right.)

- Watch 1990s movies. (This is to increase your stock of "Yo Momma" jokes.)

- Learn how to play fantasy football—your career could depend on it!

- Search the internet about international marriage law (just in case one of those online dating sites pays off).

- Register for Facebook. (What, you're not already on Facebook?!)

- Talk to your spouse. (No, I mean actually have a conversation on some meaningful topic with him or her.)

- Complete at least one task on your spouse's annoying to-do list. (It's just going to get longer while you're gone. Don't think that because you're gone, he/she is going to find a way to do everything. Guys, somehow your wife will manage to be busy the whole year.)

- Hire a landscaper/snow removal service while you are gone. (Hey, Rear D: stay away from my wife!)

- Go for a drive. (A long drive down a peaceful highway while listening to soft music—because that's the last time for 12 months you'll actually enjoy driving.)

- Spend time with your kids. (Even if that means watching *Dora the Explorer*, because you'll miss it. You may even find yourself singing the theme song: "Come on, vamanos, Everybody let's go, Come on let's get to it, You know that you can do it, Where are we going? Kabul. Where are we going? Kabul.")

- Eat at your favorite restaurant. (And hold onto that memory of what good food tastes like.)

- Take a bath. (Make it the longest, hottest bath possible, complete with Mr. Bubble, by candlelight. Later, you'll find yourself fantasizing about it.)

- Consume as much alcohol as you safely can. (Get tore up from the floor up! Stop short of throwing up on the carpet or running around the block naked wearing your army combat helmet [ACH] while singing Lee Greenwood's "I'm Proud to be an American.")

1E: Packing List

- Three dozen of Mom's chocolate chip cookies. ('Nuff said.)

- Camera (for "cool guy" pictures).

- 100 mph tape (to tape new lieutenant to cot).

- Lotion (for . . . um . . . various reasons).

- Undergarment/t-shirt sprayed with perfume/cologne of your significant other. (It could be a very long deployment!)

- Plastic baggies (because sand gets into everything).

- Baby wipes (to help stay clean and because sand gets into everything).

- Vomit bag (for C-130 plane trip).

- Noise-canceling headset (because the cheapo things they give you never work, at least for me).

- Fifty feet of 550 cord. (See **Chapter 4**).

- Excedrin. (Trust me, you'll need it.)

- Travel toothbrush, toothpaste, and deodorant (for the longest plane rides ever).

- Arabic-to-English auto-translator or pocket language guide (so you can know what your interpreter is really saying).

- Bags of snack-size candy (to bribe a local kid to keep the other kids away from your convoy or to hold you over before you can make it to the PX or care package arrives).

- iPod (for those really long convoys).

- Some form of tobacco. (Even if you don't smoke or chew now, you probably will by the end of the deployment. Even if you don't, tobacco products can be worth a lot of money, or traded for guard shifts for when you don't want to stand.)

U.S. Army Staff Sgt. Kristina Smith and her military working dog Anna search a garage suspected of being used to make vehicle-borne IEDs, June 5, 2007, in Mosul, Iraq. Smith is assigned to the 25th Infantry Division. *U.S. Air Force photo by Staff Sgt. Quinton Russ*

- Shower shoes (to protect you from all of the unidentifiable liquids, smudges, and secretions on the shower floor).

- P90X workout guide. (If your significant other leaves you, you can bulk up, look better than ever, and run over to the Sandals Resort while you're on block leave to pick up another girl.)

- A book of Chuck Norris jokes (for the commander's update brief. It will make this boring, "same deal" brief every morning seem worthwhile).

- Ear plugs (for the hideous sounds that will come from your battle buddy's side of the tent in the middle of the night).

- Stuffed animal your child gave you before you left. (Yes, before the deployment is over, you will be sleeping with it.)

- Cartoon-themed sheets for bedding and a makeshift wall. (Can you really have a bad day when the first thing you see in the morning is SpongeBob?)

- Pens, paper, and envelopes to mail letters back home saying all those things you want to say on the phone, but can't because your battle buddy is sitting next to you in the MWR tent.

1F: Tips for Packing Gear

General

- Pack bags according to unit-prescribed packing lists. If you're deploying as part of an organization and not as an individual augmentee, you might have the opportunity to place excess baggage in a container to be shipped prior to the deployment. These containers usually arrive before the first main body or shortly thereafter. It may be mandatory for you to ship one or more duffle bags of gear in these containers. If you have space left over in your duffle bags or in the container, request through your chain of command that you be allowed to ship some additional comfort items (bedding, etc.).

- Find out the total weight limit and authorized number of bags you may bring. Keep in mind that you'll have to transport your baggage from one location to another, off one chopper onto another, and from one transient tent to another, until you reach your final destination.

- If possible, make contact with the section or individual you'll be replacing downrange. Ask them about sleeping arrangements and morale centers. Is there a PX, MWR, or USO at your base? What kind of equipment (gaming systems, computers, telephones) are available at the morale centers? What kind of calling center do they have? If there's an AT&T or SPAWAR location, you can set up a SPAWAR account online over the internet or purchase AT&T calling cards prior to your departure. (Did you realize that telephone operators really exist?) Finding out as much information as you can will assist you in determining what to bring.

- Remember any professional manuals/leader's books you'll want to bring along. If possible, download them to save space; however, if you're unsure whether you'll have computer access or how often, you should bring the hard copies. There's also required documentation that you must hand-carry (soldier's counseling packets, medical records, etc.).

- Zip-Loc or resealable bags are awesome for liquids—for instance, to ensure your shampoo doesn't leak all over everything—and to serve as additional wet-weather bags.

- Your carry-on bags should have enough personal hygiene items and changes of clothing to sustain you for at least 72 hours. You might get stuck in transit at a base waiting for a flight for several days without seeing your other baggage.

Prepare for all kinds of weather, everything from extreme heat to rain and even snow. Make sure you check the airline policies for authorized items and measurement limits.

Packing the Duffle

- Place heavy or bulky items (extra boots, manuals) at the bottom to create a stable base.

- Fill the middle with clothing items in Ziploc bags or your wet-weather bag. Fold each item in half, then start rolling it at one end like a sleeping bag. Slip the items into the bag lengthwise, as tight as possible. Roll together either thin items, such as underwear, or a day's worth of clothing (one t-shirt, one pair of socks, and one set of undergarments).

- Use all available space. As you're packing, it doesn't hurt to put a boot in it—literally. Step down firmly inside your duffle to get rid of any excess space.

- Try to distribute the weight equally as you pack. Your duffle should not be lopsided or lumpy.

- Tie down all attachments and tape down excess cords/clips. For instance, if your packing list mandates that you attach your assault pack to your rucksack, make sure it's attached securely.

- Label all your gear with your name, at a minimum. Have your name sewn onto your bags or stenciled onto the bottom of your duffle bag, because velcro can easily come off or be taken off; if you use it as your only form of identification, your bags can easily get mixed up or stolen. Some units require additional marking like green tape on all of the handles in order to easily identify your unit's baggage among the rest.

Financial Matters

2A: Deployment Entitlements

♀

This information came from myarmybenefits.us.army.mil, which provides updated benefit information, including several benefit calculators.

- **Hazardous Duty Incentive Pay (HDIP)** – Soldiers who perform hazardous duties such as parachute jumping, explosives demolition, or toxic fuels handling are eligible for HDIP. The rate is $150 per month. Soldiers performing High-Altitude, Low-Opening parachute duty are eligible for $225 per month. Soldiers under competent order to participate in regular and frequent aerial flights as crew or non-crew members may be entitled to HDIP for flying duty. Officers, including aviation cadets, entitled to Aviation Career Incentive Pay (ACIP) are not entitled to HDIP for flying duty. The level of HDIP is based on pay grade and can vary from $150-$250 a month. A soldier entitled to HDIP who is hospitalized for a wound or injury incurred as a result of hostile action, or incurs a wound, injury or illness in a combat operation or combat zone designated by the Secretary of Defense, and is hospitalized outside of the theater for treatment is entitled to HDIP for 12 months.

- **Hardship Duty Pay-Location (HDP-L)** – If you are deployed to a designated hardship duty location for 30 consecutive days, on the 31st day you become entitled to retroactive HDP-L dating to the first day you reported for duty in the location. HDP-L is paid in monthly increments of $50, $100, or $150 depending on the location.

- **Hostile Fire Pay/Imminent Danger Pay (HFP/IDP)** – To receive HFP/DIP, you must be deployed to an eligible location. The Secretary of Defense has designated approximately 27 locations around the world as IDP areas. The entitlement starts upon arrival to the authorized location and terminates upon departure. Formerly you would receive $225 a month for each month, or part of a month, in which you were present in the HFP/IDP area. However, a new law may affect the pay you receive when you are on duty in an IDP area. The National Defense Authorization Act for fiscal year 2012 (NDAA 2012), signed on December 31, 2011, requires we begin prorating IDP so that members are only paid for the actual days they perform duty in an IDP area. Before December 31, members received the full $225 a month, even if they performed duty only one day in an IDP area. Now service members receive $7.50 for each day on duty in an IDP area up to the maximum monthly rate of $225. However, as the years progress these rules/laws will more than likely change so for more exact figure's ensure you check with the command or online for the most recent HFP/DIP figures.

- **Family Separation Allowance (FSA)** – While you are deployed, you are eligible for FSA when you are involuntarily separated from your dependents or active-duty spouse for more than 30 days. Service members currently drawing FSA will continue to do so during deployment. Temporary visits are authorized after the member is separated from the Permanent Duty Station (PDS).

- **Combat Zone Tax Exempt (CZTE)** – If you are receiving HFP because of assignment to a combat zone, your pay will be tax exempt. All enlisted soldiers and warrant officers are exempt from federal income tax on basic pay, jump pay, HDP, and HFP. Commissioned officers are exempt from federal income tax on amounts up to the basic pay of the senior-most enlisted, plus the amount of HFP for any qualifying month. Accrued leave sold while in a CZTE area, whether earned in that area or not, is tax exempt. Leave accrued while serving in a CZTE area, which remains unused at separation, is also tax exempt. When tax exempt leave is taken, taxable wages are reduced on W-2 wage and tax statements at the end of the tax year, based on the number of days members earned while in a combat zone.

• **Per Diem** – While on an overseas deployment, you are entitled to Outside Contiguous United States (OCONUS) incidental per diem at $3.50 a day, or $105 a month. This money is paid out for each day you are deployed, if the deployment is longer than 30 days. Per diem pay usually shows up when you return home.

• **Special Leave Accrual (SLA)** – If you are deployed in an area in which you were entitled to HFP/IDP for at least 120 continuous days, you are authorized to carry up to 90 days of leave at the end of the fiscal year. SLA must be used before the end of the third fiscal year after the fiscal year in which the qualifying service ended. The Servicemember's Civil Relief Act of 2003 (SCRA) formerly known as the Soldiers and Sailors Civil Relief Act of 1940 (SSCRA), is a federal law that gives all military members some important rights as they enter active duty. For more information about the SCRA and your rights under one of the several categories of service, please consult myarmybenefits.us.army.mil/Home?Benefit_Library/ Federal_Benefits_Page/Servicemembers_Civil_Relief_Act_ (SCRA).html.

2B: Finance/Budget Planner

The root of most family problems during a service member's deployment is usually money. Most of these problems can easily be prevented by laying out and following a good financial plan.

Here's a really basic layout that anyone can use as is or adapt as they see fit. However, no matter how good your plan, before the service member deploys, clear communication on your shared approach to finances should be established between all applicable parties.

Entitlements

Basic pay:
Basic Allowance for Housing (BAH):   _____
Basic Allowance for Substance (BAS):   _____
HFP: _____
FSA: _____
CZTE: _____
Total Pay: _____

Bills back home

Rent: _____
Car payment: _____
Utilities: _____
Cell phone: _____
Insurance: _____
Other: _____
Investments/savings: _____
Total Bills: _____

Total Pay – Total Bills = Net Pay. Make smart choices with your net pay and follow the financial plan you established before you deployed, making sure you discuss all financial decisions with applicable family members.

A piece of advice for all you young guys out there: better to choose a high-end sports car than a hot girl. The odds are the car will require less maintenance and cause fewer headaches. I realize new "toys" of any kind are always fun; but stay away from the "shiny new" girl. If you pick the car, your stress levels will be MUCH lower—trust me.

2C: Bill Tracker

Company Name	Purpose	Account Number	Username/ Password	Amount Due	Date Due	Comments

Support from Others

3A: Suggested Care Package Items

♀

When we're deployed to a theater of operation, mailings from loved ones mean a lot to us. Letters and care packages from the "civilized" world let us know we're not forgotten and that America supports us. You may not agree with the politics that surround a particular conflict, but remember that we soldiers have nothing to do with those issues.

You don't have to send fancy gadgets or spend your entire paycheck on an entire company of soldiers. Many soldiers, like me, enjoy "pen pal" relationships with the American people. It's a great way for you to show your support, and does not cost much to send a letter or email.

The following lists are suggested/requested items from fellow service members in both Iraq and Afghanistan. The lists are not all-inclusive, so don't feel limited to these items. Whatever you send will be warmly received and greatly appreciated.

Food

As you read earlier in the book, the Army provides us with three meals a day. I learned from an early age that just because food is free doesn't mean it's good. Some of you, like me, may have had some experience with government assistance in the past. If so, you know that the cheese from one of those government blocks makes one awesome grilled cheese sandwich!

However, every now and again as a child it was a nice to have McDonald's. Even as grown-up soldiers, we get sick of DFAC food all day, every day, even though it's free. We miss home-cooked meals and our favorite restaurants. Yes, in some locations downrange you can find American restaurants, but the food there doesn't taste the same. So, rather than eat Friday's surf and turf (which I affectionately refer to as "near steak") at the DFAC, I would often opt for a Cup [of] Noodles instead. Some examples of food items to send include:

- Baked goods (nothing is better than Grandma's cookies!)

- Ramen or Cup [of] Noodles

- Crackers

- Hot sauce (any flavor, but unique ones are always a treat, such as "Hot A**" sauce)

- Cocoa (during the winter months, everyone—even the "hardest" of warriors—loves an occasional cup of hot cocoa)

- Coffee

- Granola bars

- Instant oatmeal (individual packages work best)

- Candy

- Cookies

- Jerky

- Smoked meats

- Ravioli/chili (or any food product in a can that can be opened without a can opener)

- Popcorn

Entertainment

It's surprisingly easy to lose track of the days of the week. Many soldiers are avid readers of entertainment magazines such as *People* or *US Weekly*. Reading or playing simple games are excellent ways for deployed soldiers to escape the day-to-day grind. Some simple items to send soldiers include:

- Magazines

- Books

- Puzzle books, i.e., Sudoku

- Playing cards

- Board games

- Video/computer games

- Coloring books with pencils and crayons (don't laugh: some soldiers still enjoy coloring pictures to pass the time)

- DVDs or CDs

- Disposable cameras

- Stationery

- Recreational items (flying disc, football, soccer ball, hacky sack, etc.)

Seasonal items

- Holiday cookies

- Any items wrapped in seasonal wrapping paper (During one deployment I received some common items as gifts from a sponsor. They were wrapped in Christmas wrapping paper. It didn't matter to me that the items were ordinary; it was just nice to receive wrapped presents for Christmas.)

- Holiday greeting cards (both filled out by you and blank cards for the service members to send to their loved ones)

- Plastic masks at Halloween (Many FOBs celebrate holidays by running. During one Halloween run we were allowed to dress up in costumes. But even with a vivid imagination, it's hard to make a costume from almost nothing.)

- Holiday movies and specials (Besides apple pie and Elvis, what's more American than the *Peanuts* holiday specials? I received *A Charlie Brown Christmas* in a care package during one deployment. I loaned my DVD to a dozen different soldiers, both male and female, who made copies to watch on Christmas day.)

Practical items

- Wipes/moist cloths

- Hygiene items (toothpaste, dental floss, toothbrushes, razors, deodorant, feminine hygiene products, etc.)

- Eye drops

- Environmental items (sunblock, lip balm, etc.)

- Plain white socks

- Quilts/fleeces (We do have our military-issue sleeping bags, but having civilian bedding is a luxury.)

Don't

- Send baked goods if you are not a family member. Soldiers have to be careful, so it's likely the food will be thrown away uneaten.

- Send prohibited or hazardous items such as alcohol, tobacco, or pornography.

- Send weapons or ammunition of any kind.

- Send anything that's pressurized, e.g., energy drinks, shaving cream, or soda.

- Send military-issue clothing, e.g., socks, boots, etc. All soldiers are provided with what they need to make mission. We're given a clothing allowance and a deployment issue, and we can do exchanges or orders through the supply system for more items. In addition, what you send may be non-regulation items that service members cannot wear.

3B: Mailing Tips

- Use the service member's full name. Addressing mail to "Any Service Member" is no longer permitted.

- Include the unit and APO/FPO/DPO (Air/Army Post Office or Fleet Post Office) address, with the nine-digit ZIP code, if one is assigned.

Examples

SFC Kristina Smith
Unit Name
FOB Whatever
APO AE 93700-2050

SPC Joe Jones
CMR 1234
APO AA 09045-2000

Seaman Jolene Doe
USCGC George Bush
FPO AP 96668-3139

- Write your name and return address information in the upper-left corner of the shipping label.

- Weigh and measure your package before mailing. Packages sent to service members overseas cannot exceed 70 pounds and have maximum length restrictions as well, depending on the area.

- Check with your local post office for updated mailing information before you send a letter or package to a service member overseas and be aware of customs regulations for incoming mail for that region. Generally, the following are prohibited in Islamic countries:

  - Obscene articles (magazines, films, etc.).
  - Anything depicting nude or seminude persons, pornographic or sexual items.
  - Non-authorized political materials.
  - Pork or pork byproducts.
  - Bulk quantities of religious materials contrary to the Islamic faith; items for personal use of the addressee are permissible.
  - Firearms
  - Alcohol

- Pack wisely and consider how outside conditions may affect the contents of your package, for example:

  - Extreme temperatures can affect food items.
  - Inconsiderate shippers can damage the contents of your package by tossing it around, so pack fragile items in bubble wrap.
  - Liquids can leak, so place them in a plastic bag.
  - Food can contaminate other items, so try to separate those items from hygiene items. (I once received a package that had unpacked fabric softener sheets in the same package

as baked goods that were wrapped only in plastic wrap. Everything smelled liked fabric softener.)

• Inconsistent mail service can affect delivery times, so allow sufficient time for the package to get overseas—up to six weeks, or even longer.

3C: Making Phone Calls from Abroad

The following information came from the Defense Information Systems Agency (DISA) at www.disa.mil.

Voice Telephone Calls (DSN)

Voice telephone calls can access a Defense Switched Network (DSN) line by either direct dialing or dialing the operator. Here's how each process works:

You dial

• Listen for the dial tone.

• Dial the DSN access number, if required.

• Listen for the DSN dial tone.

• Dial the DSN phone number, with precedence and area code, if required.

The operator dials

• Give your name and local base telephone extension number.

• Give your precedence.

• Provide the DSN number you are calling and any other information.

- Wait on the line until the operator connects you to the called party.

Calls to Commercial Numbers

Official long-distance calls may be placed using a combination of DSN and local base switchboard lines. When authorized by the local commander's policy, base switchboard operators may connect incoming DSN calls to a local commercial number if the called commercial number is within the toll-free radius of the switchboard. Off-net operations are at the day-by-day discretion of local base officials. Due to the possibility of abuse and difficulty of control, the automatic completion of on-off-net calls is not authorized. Although DSN off-net capability exists at many military installations, DISA does not provide off-net directory service for official calls.

Call Assistance

Switchboard operators are available to assist DSN users. If you are having trouble completing a call, dial 312-560-1110 to reach the operator.

Inter-Area Calling

- The DSN provides global telephone service for authorized users. Some users can call everywhere, while others are limited to one particular area or combination of areas. Where you can call depends on your mission and how your telephone line is class marked. If your calling area is limited, you will not be able to dial outside your calling area. The local directory indicates the calling areas and codes available to you.

- The area code is not needed for calls within your area. Calls to an area outside the local call boundary require an area code plus the 7-digit DSN number. If you are transmitting data, alternate area codes are used.

Calling Cards

- Dial 809-463-3376 as your DSN number when using a calling card.

- Dial the 809 number just as you would any other DSN number; wait for the second dial tone; then follow the instructions on your calling card or dial your 800 number.

- If a location/individual has an 800 number, you won't need a calling card; just dial the 809 number and wait for the dial tone, then dial your 800 number.

Only two types of calling cards: AT&T Global Calling Card and Sergovia (SPAWAR) are guaranteed to work in deployed areas. Depending on where you are, one or both will be available. Many other commercial calling cards are available for purchase, but they may not work. The rates vary from card to card, brand to brand, and carrier to carrier depending on which calling card you purchase. As family members and friends of your service member, you can purchase calling cards for your soldier. If you do, ensure you mail or email the access number, instructions, and pin number from the card to your service member.

- AT&T Global Calling Card: These can only be purchased through the military AAFES exchange stores. If you are a family member or friend, you can purchase directly from AAFES online at https://shop.aafes.com/scs/ even if you don't have a military identification card. Friends and family back home can recharge minutes to a deployed soldier's prepaid card simply by having the soldier provide them with the 800 number and pin number located on the back of the prepaid card. Then they would call the 800 number and follow the voice prompts to add minutes. The cost is approximately $0.39/minute. These are from regular landline phones at the AT&T calling centers. AT&T Global Calling Cards are offered in two increments of 550-minute or 300-minute cards.

When you buy a Global Calling Card in the U.S., but use it overseas, the rates will be higher, so you won't get nearly as many minutes.

-   A 550-minute card has 550 minutes of state-to-state calling, but only 146 minutes for calls from Iraq, Kuwait, or Afghanistan to the U.S. One card costs $22.

-   Similarly, a 300-minute card has 78 minutes for calls from Iraq, Kuwait, or Afghanistan calling to the U.S. One card costs $15.

•   AT&T Ship-to-Shore Calling Cards. This is the only prepaid card that can be used on board Navy ships and Coast Guard cutters. You also have international access to over 200 countries worldwide. The price to call from U.S. Navy ships via AT&T's Direct Ocean Services (DOS) to the U.S. is approximately $0.50/minute; however, the call dollar amount varies by call location.

•   SPAWAR Calling Cards: These use voice over internet protocol (VOIP) lines, via a computer connection. These cards can only be purchased by setting up an account with SPAWAR online at http://icpaccess.net/. A family member can set up the account for the soldier. The cost is approximately $0.04/minute.

-   On at least two days of every month, deployed service members can make calls to the U.S.A., its territories, or to landlines in other military home base countries from their local SPAWAR internet cafe at no cost. There are no hidden fees or restrictions on these free call days; all calls on these days are FREE from midnight to midnight, EST.

-   The "Free Call Day" program began on Mother's Day in 2006 with the support of the Veterans of Foreign Wars (VFW) Operation Uplink Program. Until that time, Operation Uplink had distributed individual calling cards to deployed or hospitalized troops. At the start, there were only 191 SPAWAR internet cafes; since then, the network has grown to over 850 cafes located in three countries, servicing the calling needs of hundreds of thousands of troops. The network connects them to the U.S. and hundreds of other destinations around the globe. Along with this network growth, Operation Uplink's commitment to the program grew, from three days of sponsorship in 2006 to 24 days in 2011. Due to the cost effectiveness of the program, the VFW no longer provides calling cards for deployed troops, devoting 100% of their donated dollars to providing free call days to the troops on a global basis through a combination of the SPAWAR internet cafe network and DSN access to sponsored stateside calling.

Skype

Skype is the newest—and most popular—way of communicating with loved ones back home.

- Skype is a VOIP service and a division of Microsoft.

- Skype's many features include video-conferencing, short message service (SMS), voicemail, contact list, public chats, call forwarding, sketch pad, business control panel, desktop sharing, and more.

- Skype is both a free and a subscription-based internet phone service. It is free to start using Skype to speak, see, and instant message anyone who has an account on Skype, using a PC or Skype-compatible device.

- You need a computer, speakers or headphones, a microphone, an internet connection, and the Skype software, which is free to download at www.skype.com.

Pricing

- Free: Skype-to-Skype calls, one-to-one video calls, instant messaging, screen sharing.

- Pay as you go from $0.023/minute. Call phones, SMS, and call forwarding. You can add features when you need them with Skype credit.

• Subscriptions from $0.012/minute. Good for frequent calling and calling abroad. Lowest calling rates; choose unlimited calling and get the best rates with a 3- or 12-month subscription.

• Skype Premium from $4.99 to $9.99/month. You can get up to 50% off when they have specials. Unlimited calls to a country of your choice; group video calling; screen sharing; live chat customer support.

Payment methods

- Skrill is a payment provider that allows you to securely send and receive money via email. You can use Skrill in combination with your credit card, debit card, or your bank account to buy Skype credit.
- PayPal: http://www.paypal.com.
- MasterCard, VISA, or Diners Club.

3D: Organizations that Support Deployed Soldiers

The following organizations support deployed service members through either care packages or letters. If you can't find what you're looking for through the organizations listed, you can find additional agencies by searching the internet.

• A Million Thanks: www.amillionthanks.org. A year-round campaign to show appreciation for our U.S. military men and women, past and present, for their sacrifices, dedication, and service to our country through our letters, emails, cards, and prayers.

• Adopt a U.S. Soldier: www.adoptausSoldier.org. A nonprofit organization that seeks volunteers to help show the brave men and women fighting for our freedom that their sacrifices will not go unnoticed. It connects supportive civilians with deployed troops and offers a channel by which to communicate encouragement and express gratitude to those brave men and women serving in the United States armed forces.

- Any Soldier: www.anySoldier.com. Sponsors care packages to service members deployed.

- Blue Star Mothers of America, Inc.: www.bluestarmothers. org. Runs a project called Sew Much Comfort. It provides adaptive clothing free of charge to support the unique needs of our injured service members from all branches of the military and National Guard. The need for adaptive clothing continues to grow as injured American military members serving their country return to the States every week.

- Operation Paperback: www.operationpaperback.org. Operation Paperback is a non-profit organization incorporated in Pennsylvania that collects gently used books nationwide and sends them to American troops overseas, as well as veterans and military families here at home.

- Give 2 the Troops: www.give2thetroops.org. A nonpartisan, non-political, patriotic organization aimed at supporting U.S.-deployed and wounded troops in harm's way. Patriotic citizens ensure that deployed U.S. military members in all branches of service are supported with letters and care packages.

- Joining Forces: www.joiningforces.gov. A comprehensive national initiative to mobilize all sectors of society to give our service members and their families the opportunities and support they have earned. Supporting our soldiers is a priority of the White House.

- Military Missions: www.military-missions.org. A nonprofit charity organization made up of volunteers who seek to ensure that our troops, our veterans, and their families are always encouraged. The organization has a number of opportunities available that give everyone a chance to say "thank you" to our heroes. It plays the role of facilitator in a community where civilians and military personnel work and live together. As our military personnel serve, providing protection and safety for all of us, we work to give something back to our troops and their families.

• Operation Gratitude: www.opgratitude.com. Annually sends 100,000 care packages filled with snacks, entertainment items, and personal letters of appreciation addressed to individually named U.S. service members deployed in hostile regions, to their children left behind, and to wounded warriors recuperating in Transition Units. Their mission is to lift morale, bring a smile to a service member's face, and express to our armed forces the appreciation and support of the American people. Each package contains donated products valued at ~$125 and costs the organization $15 to assemble and ship. For safety and security, assembling packages occurs at the Army National Guard armory in Van Nuys, California. Since its inception in 2003, Operation Gratitude volunteers have shipped more than 750,000 packages to American military members and their children.

• Operation Shoe Box: www.operationshoebox.com. Founded in 2003 to support and raise the morale of our men and women deployed outside the USA and let them know they are appreciated. Operation Shoe Box sends care packages and letters that can be beneficial to soldiers during their deployment. The organization is composed of over 1,300 dedicated volunteers in three locations and also volunteers all across the USA.

• Operation Troop Aid (OTA): www.operationtroopaid.com Their mission is to provide care packages for U.S. service members with revenue generated from professional concert promotions and public financial generosity. OTA is a nonprofit corporation striving to make a positive difference and inspire our armed forces by letting them know Americans stand with them.

- Operation USO: www.uso.org. For 70 years, the USO has provided a tangible way for all Americans to say thank you for the dedication and sacrifice of our troops and their families. The USO fulfills its mission of lifting the spirits of America's troops and their families through an extensive range of programs at more than 160 locations in 27 states and 14 countries, and at hundreds of entertainment events each year. USO volunteers provide a home away from home for our troops to keep them connected to the families they left behind. The USO makes sure your help goes to those who need it the most: troops serving in combat, their families, our wounded warriors and their families, and families of the fallen.

- Soldier Angels: www.soldiersangels.org. A volunteer-led nonprofit providing aid and comfort to the men and women of the United States Army, Marines, Navy, Air Force, Coast Guard, and their families. Angel volunteers assist veterans, wounded soldiers, and deployed personnel and their families in a variety of unique and effective ways.

3E: Mental Health/Suicide Prevention Resources

For Immediate Help, 24/7

- Contact a consultant now: 1-800-342-9647

- International calling options:
  - Toll-Free*: 1-800-342-9647
  - En español llame al: 1-877-888-0727
  - TTY/TDD: 1-866-607-6794

- Safe Helpline – sexual assault support for the DoD community: 1-877-995-5247

- Suicide Prevention Lifeline: 1-800-273-TALK (8255)

Other Organizational Resources

- Behavior Health Professional, www.behavioralhealth.army. mil: Their efforts in education, prevention, and early treatment are unprecedented. Their goal is to ensure that every deployed and returning soldier receives the health care they need.

- The Defense Centers of Excellence for Psychological Health and Traumatic Brain Injury (DCoE)

  - Main phone number: 1-866-966-1020
  - Suicide Prevention Lifeline: 1-800-273-TALK (8255)
  - Wounded Soldier and Family Hotline: 1-800-984-8523

- Real Warriors, www.realwarriors.net: The Real Warriors Campaign is an initiative launched by DCoE to promote the processes of building resilience, facilitating recovery, and supporting reintegration of returning service members, veterans, and their families. The Real Warriors Campaign is committed to providing service members, veterans, military families and health professionals with the resources they need to overcome the barriers to care that may prevent warriors from seeking needed care for invisible wounds.

- Army Family Readiness Group (Army FRG), www.armyfrg. org: The Army FRG website provides a secure environment in which information, resources, and support are available to soldiers and their family members 24 hours a day, regardless of their geographic location. A unit's virtual FRG site, or vFRG, promotes a community feeling within Army units by providing a place that is customized to the unit and contains content that is controlled by the unit. Army FRG provides all of the functionality of a traditional FRG in an ad-hoc and online setting to meet the needs of geographically dispersed units and families across all components of the Army. Army FRG is a commander's tool that allows them to communicate directly to soldiers and family members. Unit vFRG sites can be accessed any time to view information and photos, read stories, ask questions, participate in forums, and much more.

- Military OneSource: A free service provided by the DoD to service members and their families to help with a broad range of concerns, including money management, spouse employment and education, parenting and child care, relocation, deployment, reunion, and the particular concerns of families with special-needs members. They can also address more complex issues such as relationships, stress, and grief. Services are available 24 hours a day, by telephone and online. Many Military OneSource staff members have military experience (veterans, spouses, Guardsmen, Reservists), and all receive ongoing training on military matters and the military lifestyle. The program can be especially helpful to service members and their families who live far from installations.

- Afterdeployment.org: Its mission is to provide self-care solutions targeting post-traumatic stress, depression, and other behavioral health challenges commonly faced after a deployment. Specific goals include:

    - To be the pre-eminent psychological health and traumatic brain injury (TBI) web portal serving the military community.

    - Create and provide media-rich, web-based, self-care solutions targeting mental health problems commonly faced following a deployment.

    - Conduct research and determine best practices for delivering online mental health resources to service members, their families, and veterans.

    - Develop PH/TBI standards, processes, and review mechanisms.

- Act as the DoD resource for providing pre-clinical care to warfighters and their families in the months following a deployment.

- Coordinate telehealth services to educate, prevent, screen, assess, and treat common adjustment issues.

- Train senior leadership and behavioral health providers on best practices for treatment and prevention approaches using technology.

- Offer self-care solutions for addressing mental health needs.

- Obtain resources necessary to develop new programs on an as-needed basis.

- Contacts

  - Outreach center: 866-966-1020

  - Military and veterans crisis line: 800-273-8255

- Military Family Life Consultant (MFLC): Someone who helps warriors balance the demands of a military career with family responsibilities.

  - The program offers trained, professional counselors for service members and their families to speak with. All conversations are confidential and free of charge.

  - Augments existing military support programs by providing short-term, problem-solving, non-medical counseling to service members and their families. Specially trained on military-specific topics, MFLCs provide education and information on a variety of issues that warriors and their families may face throughout the deployment cycle.

  - MFLCs are not traditional therapists; instead they help service members and military families develop an action plan for addressing problems. Sometimes called "walk-about counselors," MFLCs proactively contact warriors and family members, often in public settings such as hallways, hospitals, cafeterias, and recreational facilities.

- Through non-medical counseling, MFLCs support military families with a variety of common issues that occur within the military lifestyle, including:
  - Common stress reactions to deployment
  - Reintegration and the transition from warrior to citizen
  - Relocation adjustment
  - Separation
  - Homesickness
  - Loss or grief
  - Resiliency
  - Anxiety, sadness, or other common emotional concerns
- MFLCs are also professionally trained to provide non-medical counseling for important life skills, such as:
  - Personal financial management
  - Productivity at work
  - Parenting
  - Anger management
  - Conflict resolution
  - Decision making
  - Relationship issues
- MFLCs can talk to you in individual, couple, family, or group settings, and often have walk-in or flexible appointment times and meeting locations. Additionally, MFLCs at your installation may offer educational sessions targeting one of the specific life skills mentioned above. Finally, it's important to remember that no files or records are kept about your confidential interactions with a MFLC, which can help make the experience more comfortable.
- MFLCs and programs vary by base and installation and can be accessed through locations such as Army Community Services, Marine Corps Community Services, Navy

Fleet and Family Support Centers, or Airman and Family Readiness Centers.

- For information about Child and Youth Behavioral MFLCs—who specialize in supporting warriors with younger children—contact your installation's Family Center, Child Development Center, or school liaison officer.

Use the Following as Additional Resources

- Your family and friends

- Your chain of command

- Primary care provider

- Chaplain/Unit Ministry Team

Military Acronyms and Jargon

100 mph tape – Duct tape. The name comes from a specific variety that was used during the Vietnam War to repair helicopter rotor blades.

550 cord – Cord/twine/string with a rated strength of 550 lbs.

AAFES – Army and Air Force Exchange Service. The supporting infrastructure for PXs.

ACH – Army combat helmet.

ACU – Army combat uniform.

AK-47 – Russian-made shoulder weapon.

AKA – Also known as.

AOR – Area of responsibility.

ASPCA – American Society for the Prevention of Cruelty to Animals.

Assault pack – Army backpack.

Battle buddies – Partners, assigned to assist each other.

BDOC – Base Defense Operations Center.

Bradley – The M2 infantry fighting vehicle. Its role is to transport foot soldiers on the battlefield, to provide fire cover to dismounted troops, and to suppress enemy tanks and fighting vehicles.

CALL – Center for Army Lessons Learned.

Call sign – Code name for an individual.

CDC – Center for Disease Control and Prevention.

Chain of command – The line of authority and responsibility along which orders are passed within a military unit. You have a boss, who has a boss, and his boss is your boss' boss.

Chaplain – The go-to guy for all religious needs.

Chopper – Helicopter.

Chow – Food.

CHU – Containerized Housing Unit. Living quarters consisting of a steel container with a door and sometimes windows.

Code word – A replacement name for something secret.

Coin – A verb, as in to coin. A way to reward soldiers for excellence. Their command team presents them with a specially made commemorative coin.

Combat landing – A descent an aircraft makes to a landing strip, usually fast and dramatic.

Combat Stress – A place soldiers can go downrange for conversation or counseling if they're feeling overwhelmed by the combat environment.

Commo – Communications, as in "the commo guy".

Connex – A big, metal, rectangular-shaped box. Used to ship almost everything for a deployment.

Convoy – Multiple vehicles closely following each other to a set destination.

COP – Combat outpost.

CSM – Command sergeant major.

CZTE – Combat Zone Tax Exempt.

DFAC (pronounced "dee-fak") – Dining facility, or Army cafeteria.

DoD – Department of Defense.

Downrange – Forward deployed area.

DSN – Defense Switched Network; for making voice telephone calls from abroad.

Duffle bag – Large, green packing bag, in which all Army gear gets stored when on the move.

ECP – Entry control point.

First Sergeant – A senior enlisted rank; E-8.

FOB – Forward operating base.

Fobbit – A combination of the acronym FOB and the term Hobbit from Tolkien's *The Lord of the Rings* series. Applied to personnel who remain on base and don't venture outside the wire on missions.

FRG – Family Readiness Group.

FSA – Family Separation Allowance.

FSG – Family support group.

FUD – Female urination device. Allows a female soldier to urinate while standing up, without exposing herself.

GP – General purpose.

Gun bunny – Combat arms soldier.

Handle – Pseudonym used by radio operators. Similar to a call sign.

HDIP – Hazardous duty incentive pay.

HDP-L – Hardship Duty Pay-Location.

HFP – Hostile fire pay.

HMMWV (pronounced "hum-vee") – High Mobility Multipurpose Wheeled Vehicle. Replacement for the WWII-era jeep.

"Hooah" – The all-purpose Army reply; also used for emphasis or agreement.

IDF – Indirect fire.

IED – Improvised explosive device.

ISSO – Information systems security officer.

JST – Joint Services Transcript.

Kennel master – The boss of all the military working dog teams.

Kilometer – The unit of distance everyone uses except us Yanks. Equivalent to a little over six-tenths of a mile.

Latrine – Restroom/outhouse.

LES – Leave and earnings statement.

MFLC – Military family life consultant.

MOS – Military occupational specialty.

MP – Military Police.

MRAP – Mine-resistant, ambush-protected vehicle.

MRE – Meal, ready to eat. Like sack lunches for soldiers.

MWD – Military working dog.

MWR – Morale, welfare, and recreation.

NATO – North Atlantic Treaty Organization.

NCO – Non-commissioned officer. Enlisted ranks between E-4 and E-10.

Non/less than lethal rounds – Rubber bullets or beanbags.

Outside the wire – Beyond the confines of the compound.

Patrol base – A position a squad or platoon conducting a patrol sets up when it halts for an extended period.

Patrol cap – Army baseball-like hat.

PCS – Permanent change of station. Used as both a noun and a verb.

PEDD – Patrol explosive detection dog.

PT – Physical training.

PTSD – Post-traumatic stress disorder.

Puddle jumper – Very small plane.

PX – Post exchange. A small "department store" on a military base.

QRF – Quick Reaction Force.

Quid pro quo – Latin phrase meaning "this for that"—an exchange.

The rear – Back home.

Rear D/Detachment – A very small contingent of your unit who are left behind to handle a variety of tasks after you deploy.

RIP – Relieve/relief in place.

Sandbox – Deployment areas of Middle Eastern countries.

Sarge – Informal for "Sergeant," applicable to many NCOs.

SFC – Sergeant First Class. An E-7.

SGLI – Servicemembers Group Life Insurance.

SHARP – Sexual Harassment/Assault Response Prevention.

SLA – Special Leave Accrual.

SME – Subject matter expert.

SOP – Standard operating procedure.

SPAWAR – Space and Naval Warfare Systems Command; runs an international phone calling service.

SRC – Soldier readiness checklist/center.

Staff Judge Advocate – The office that provides legal services to Army soldiers.

TCP – Traffic control point. A form of manned roadblock.

Terp – Language interpreter.

Theater of operation – A region in which active military operations are in progress.

TOA – Transfer of authority.

Tracer rounds – Special rounds inserted into ammunition belts every certain number of rounds. They light up when fired and are visible in flight, allowing the gunner to adjust his aim.

TTP – Techniques, tactics, and procedures.

T-wall – A tall, free-standing, concrete panel with a footing cast into the base. Used in combination to protect bases, buildings, and personnel.

UAV – Unmanned aerial vehicle.

USO – United Services Organization.

VBIED – vehicle-borne improvised explosive device.

VTC – Video teleconference.

WMR – Welfare, meals, recreation center.

WTH – "What the (heck)."

Index

Stars and Stripes, 97

About the Authors

Paul Smith joined the army in 2005 and served as a Signal Support Systems Specialist. During his active duty period he was stationed at Fort Carson, Colorado and deployed from there to Iraq in 2008-2009. After Paul got out of the army in 2011, he stayed in Colorado Springs and pursued contracting work overseas which allows him to continue to actively serve U.S. forces in Afghanistan.

Sergeant First Class Kristina Smith is currently serving as a platoon sergeant stationed at Fort Drum, New York. She joined the U.S. Army in June 1996 in her hometown of Marshalltown, Iowa and has continued to serve on active duty since. Her assignments include Fort Polk, Louisiana; Hanau, Germany; Fort Knox, Kentucky; Camp Red Cloud, South Korea; Baumholder, Germany; Fort Sill, Oklahoma; and now Fort Drum, New York. She has deployed to both Iraq and Afghanistan. Kristina has also served in support of Operation Northern Watch. SFC Smith has received numerous awards and accolades over her career. She is a former U.S. Army Drill Sergeant who graduated as a member of the Commandant's list at the U.S. Army Drill Sergeant School at Fort Jackson, South Carolina. She was selected as the Distinguished Leadership Graduate of her PLDC Class 08-01 and graduated as a member of the Commandant's list of her SLC Class 002-11. She was selected as the 21st Theater Support Command Soldier of the Year 2001 in U.S. Army Europe. She was also selected as the Division Level II NCO of the 2nd QTR FY 05 by the 17th Aviation Brigade in United States Forces Korea. She is the proud mother of her teenage son Daniel. Her family enjoys traveling to new and exciting places.